A Star Is Born!

PD the Pug on the Silver Screen

By PD the Pug
(With help from Mommy Marilee Joyce)

Illustrations by Maria Vyasene

Printed in the United States of America
Paperback ISBN: 978-1-961624-99-3
Ebook ISBN: 979-8-9877116-8-2

www.DartFrogBooks.com

To all the casting agents
who are vying for the
privilege of representing me.

INTRODUCTION

At the time of this writing, there are 2,772 stars on the Hollywood Walk of Fame.

Each year, more than ten million visitors flock to this historic landmark in Hollywood, California, to gaze upon these five-pointed terrazzo and brass tributes, these monuments to the achievements of those in the entertainment industry.

The stars—which are roughly three feet across and two inches deep—include the names of actors, directors, producers, singers, musical groups and others in the celebrity business. The Walk of Fame lines fifteen blocks of Hollywood Boulevard and three blocks of Vine Street. To walk the entire Walk, you would have to traipse more than three miles.

According to the Hollywood Chamber of Commerce, approximately twenty new stars are added to the Walk of Fame every year—twenty stars honoring the most talented, most gifted, most accomplished, most masterful, most phenomenal, only the classiest of class acts. Those honored on the Walk are the envy of their peers, recognized as having "made it" in the performance world.

And this year, one of those stars will bear the name PD THE PUG.

That's because I am about to become a big movie star!

Like a matinee idol of old, PD the Pug soon will be a megastar, a superstar, a household name. I'll be the main attraction, the top banana, the headliner, the epitome of excellence on the big screen.

A Movie Star! Me!

Um, okay, so maybe you don't know my name just *yet*, and maybe that's because this is just my first film, and maybe, um, I'm just an *extra*. But still! Superstardom is my destiny!

When Mommy saw the online advertisement seeking two dog extras for a Chewy Productions film, she must have known our financial ship had come in. I mean, look at me! This mug was made for the movies. Mommy filled out the online application and attached the required headshot. A couple of months later, the Chewy Corporation called with the great news that I was one of the two dogs chosen! I couldn't hear the other end of the call, but undoubtedly the Chewy person was telling Mommy that she clearly has a soon-to-be Hollywood icon living under her roof.

So tomorrow we are off to the filming location that will go down in history as the place where PD the Pug began his acting career. This production's location one day will be a major reason tourists flock to the DC area. Tour guides will point out the turf I trod, the trees I marked, the holes I dug. PD fans will take pictures of one another posing this way and that next to a life-size PD cardboard cutout. Mommy will watch and rewatch the PD documentary about my stardom and remember so fondly the place where it all began.

But that's later! Tomorrow, this future heartthrob and all the other extras go to the production set for day one of the shoot. And while my script might say "Extra," your pal PD is no one-in-a-crowd canine. Obviously, once Mr. Chewy meets me and observes my acting chops, he will award me a much more prominent role.

So tomorrow is it: my introduction to film fame and fortune. Soon, I will be sought after for endorsement deals from dog food companies, dog toy manufacturers, PetSmart, PetCo, Loyal Companion—even the crème de la crème, Arlington's own Woof Gang Dog Bakery, home of my beloved frosted dog cookies.

Stardom . . . mine! And then that call from the Hollywood Chamber to attend the unveiling of my Star.

Thus far, only three dogs have received a cherished star on the Hollywood Walk of Fame: Strongheart, Rin Tin Tin and Lassie.

Well, move over, Strongheart. Step aside, Rin Tin Tin. Hold my nonalcoholic dog beer, Lassie.

PD the Pug: box office gold!

Nothing can dim this rising star . . . right??

(PD note: Asta and Toto were robbed.)

Chapter One

MR. CHEWY, I'M READY FOR MY CLOSE-UP

Mommy is not too awful at this exercise called Pilates. It's a mind/body workout that was invented in the early 20th century by a German physical trainer named Joseph Pilates. It involves about fifty movements that focus on working the muscles, improving endurance, posture, balance and flexibility.

A big component of the workout is what the Pilates people call "the Pilates breath," which is described as a deep inhale through the nose with an exhale through the mouth. Pilates breathing includes diaphragmatic breathing and lateral breathing; both types cause efficient, effective respiration.

As of this writing, Pilates has more than twelve million practitioners. Lord Almighty, I wish I were one of them. Because right now my breathing is anything but efficient or effective. I am miles past panting. Far beyond wheezing and gasping. I am hyperventilating like I'd be if I ever saw Ralph hitting on my secret fawn girl pug crush.

I'm seeing stars, and not like the ones on the Hollywood Walk, either. Nope, these are the stars you see right before those cartoon birds whirl in circles around your head and you pass out and splat on the ground and then the ambulance comes and you go to Caring Hands Animal Hospital in Clarendon, where Dr. Bush did the Bad Surgery (see all three of my prior books).

"PD? PD! What's the matter, honey?" We have just arrived at the filming location, and Mommy has that concerned look about her like the time my throw-up was orange and she noticed pieces of orange yarn in the yucky and said I should be more mindful of what I ingest on walkies. Pointing to the guest seating area not far from the set for today's shoot, she continues: "Sweetie, this is as far as I can go because family can't be on set with the cast, but I'll be right over there cheering you on, okay?"

Casting my googly eyes from a walking-away-Mommy to the cast with whom I soon will be showing my movie acting mastery, I square my broad shoulders and take a deep inhalation like I'm Mommy in a Level III Pilates class. *In* through the flat nose . . . *Out* through the jutted jaw. Control the *wheeze*. Control the *snort*. Control the *grunt*. Easy peasy, PD. You got this. Act the part: calm, controlled canine. Act the part: peerless pug on the path to motion picture preeminence. You're an *actor*! *Act*!!

And I still am pinching myself about the fact that I *really am* an actor, that true fame is just around the corner. Soon I will be guesting on talk shows, and appearing at all the special events promoting my film. Yes, *my* film! PD the Pug: *starring* in a major motion picture. Extra, schmextra! The minute I show everybody my method, my moxie, my mastery of all things movie, I'll take my rightful place at the top of the marquee.

The film in which I am getting my big break is called *A Bone to Pick*. Even though it isn't about a bone like the ones I enjoy gnawing on, just having the word *bone* in the title is a sign from the heavens that this movie was made for me, made to launch my thespian career, set sail to the line of business—*show* business—for which I was born.

I don't know much about the movie's plot; the ad Mommy responded to apparently didn't give much away about the storyline. But I did hear her on the phone with Uncle Robbie telling him that the film's full title is *A Bone to Pick: Vexation Vengeance* and that the Googly search she did said it's about some guy's grudge against an unscrupulous double-dealer and the guy's plan for revenge . . . probably like my own grudge against that mangy mongrel Ralph (see all my prior books) and my own fantasies about how to vanquish him once and for all.

Bringing my thoughts back to the immediate acting I need to do, I strut toward a table with a sign that reads "Extras—Collect Scripts Here." I take my place at the back of a longish line and imperceptibly hang my round head in pity for these minor players, these mere extras, these unimportant backgrounders around me.

True, right *now,* for this short moment, I might be just an extra, just a little black ball of fur among dozens of other smalltimers. But by the time this flick hits the cinema, my name will be known by every director and production house in America and even overseas! Soon, *very* soon, it will be me, my name on the marquee.

That's because I know just what to do to so outshine these other unknowns that I will be catapulted from nobody to somebody. From extra to most-ra!

While I wait in line, I think about my plan. You see, sometimes after Mommy goes to the movies, I hear her tell a friend that one of the lesser-known actors "really made the film"—meaning he or she did something that really stood out, and even though the part was small, the performance was huge. That is going to be *me*! Years from now, people will say this is the film that kicked off the stardom of PD the Pug, Hollywood heartthrob.

That's because I'm going to be one of those actors who stands out—and I know just how do it.

The plan came to me early this morning as Mommy dried me from the icky bath she gave me so I would be all clean-smell when I arrived on set. Trying to focus on anything but being a miserable soapy wet dog, my mind went to my forthcoming star on the Walk and then to the movie that will get me there, and *that* made me think of its title:

A Bone to Pick.

And then *that* made me think of bones, and how yummy bones are, and how much fun it is to gnaw on them—even if they are those "recreational dog bones" and not the cooked bones that Mommy says are a no-no for me and other canines. Between bones and bully sticks, I could gnaw and gnaw and gnaw for hours. Unfortunately, the Warden (i.e., Mommy) generally allows me to munch and masticate for only thirty or so minutes a day.

But instead of feeling growly at her about it, I am sending Mommy a mental tail wag as I think back on my entrepreneurial idea. Her refusal to let me quickly gnaw through my bones, her insisting we "save some for later," is going to help me catapult from unknown to most-known member of this movie's entire cast.

My plan is as simple as it is profound. The name of the film is *A Bone to Pick,* right? Well, what better weapon for the hero to wield than a bone? It's hard enough to administer a nice pounding, *and* it can serve a marketing purpose! Can't you just see the movie poster? The big star brandishing a bone at the bad guy! Probably with *me*—now a member of the main cast—somewhere in the advert!

All I needed for my plan was a bone to take with me to the shoot. Mommy always keeps my partially-chewed ones in the treat cabinet. So, early this morning when she was upstairs getting better-looking for today's exciting event, I scurried over to the treat cabinet, nosed it open enough to get a paw in and felt around. Luckily there were a few bones to choose from, and I found an absolute *beaut*: a gorgeous femur bone that was barely chewed and retained its original perfect bone shape.

I then took the Kong lunchbox that Mommy packed with kibble and about a fourth of one of Great Auntie Sheila's frosted dog cookies, and—with herculean mental and emotional courage—emptied it out to make room for the secret weapon that is going to result in my rapid rise to cinematic celebrity. PD the Pug is just an hour or so away from going from unknown backgrounder to *Star!*

My plan would not have worked if the studio provided free lunch to backgrounders like me. Only those farther up the food chain, so to speak, get to partake in the spread of catered yummies at the craft services table. As an extra (for now), I have to bring my own lunch—and my Kong lunch box is the perfect way to smuggle in the bone I intend to proffer as the hero's weapon. Since most of the other extras likewise are schlepping supper in some type of lunch pail or tote, my bone-concealing Kong box doesn't arouse any suspicion. So I am able to have my secret weapon at the ready.

I should note that my idea is made yet more impressive when you consider the sacrifice I made so that I would be able to put my plan into action. See, we pug dogs are what's called "food-motivated." So Mommy would nearly faint to learn that I traded *lunch* for stardom. I love food more than most anything. I mean, honestly, I mostly think about two things during the day: 1) Food, and 2) My secret fawn girl pug crush . . . and I will be so sorry to one day admit to her that that is the order of my desires (although as a pug herself, I am guessing she will admit that her own list resembles mine).

The *point* is that if I was willing to go sans lunch on a day as important as this one, you can bet it is for a good reason. And my reason is nothing short of attaining stardom. My brainstorm is brilliant. My star on the Walk is a done deal.

Yep, as soon as I hear the *CLAP!* of the clapperboard and the director yell "Action!," I will implement my plan and get a paw up on the crowd of extras around me. My idea is pure genius! I'm sure to capture the attention of the director and other higher-ups here on the set, and maybe even Mr. Chewy himself when he hears from his underlings that I not only shine as an actor but also can improvise and add that extra sumpin-sumpin to a movie.

While the extras around me will be lucky if they ever get even another background role, I am about to be slingshotted from unsung to celebrated, from the minors to the majors, to enjoy all the fortune that comes with fame. Mommy and I will be living the life that pugs—which in ancient days were the companions of Chinese royalty, kept in luxury and guarded by troops—deserve to enjoy.

"Attention! Attention, everyone," says a middle-aged man into a megaphone, snapping me out of my royalty day-dream. His name badge tells us he is *Matt, Assistant Director.* He announces, "It's time to shoot our first extras' scene. Please leave your lunches on the long table at the back of the set, and then follow me."

I go with the group but carefully conceal my Kong pail on the non-Matt side of my dark body. I walk close to two short people, hoping this will help conceal the fact that I still have my banned box with me as we turn around and wait for our assistant director's next directive. I know Mommy would issue me a ten-minute time-out in my crate if she knew I was disobeying my boss, but I am not fretting over that because I know she will be so happy with me for my ingenuity when she is living off the largesse of my star salary and residuals, laden down with bling and wearing only designer brands as she entertains her envious friends in our mansion.

"Okay, before we start today's shoot, I need to lay out a few ground rules," Matt says. "You are the chosen, the ones who made the cut and now get to be in a major motion picture. But with that privilege come some important responsibilities that I need all of you to take very seriously."

Geesh, what a buzzkill, I think as I sit on my lunchbox so it can't be seen from Matt's post at the front of this assemblage. *Can we just get going with the first take so I can get reassigned from the riffraff to be with the actors of repute—the ones who really rank?* I hardly need to learn Matt's laws for the lessers. The sooner we get to the extra-ing, the sooner I can unveil my smart scheme and be recognized as—and rewarded for exhibiting skills befitting—the amazing actor I am.

"First," drones Matt, "as you will note in your scripts, you are in the background. *Background,* for our purposes today, is defined as the people who blend into a scene. *Background* means you are part of a crowd, and even if you are near the mains—the real stars, or just other actors more important than you—you are not the focus. At all. Bear that in mind. You are *nameless* and *interchangeable.* That means *replaceable.* So no improv, please. No going off script. No ad-libbing. No anything that calls attention to you and away from what we want our audience to be focused on."

I can't wait to fire this guy, I fume as I consider getting out my secret weapon now just to waggle it in front of his nose and make clear to this temporary taskmaster that I am not long for this extras game. But he is not worth the risk of this choice bone getting taken away from me before I can use it and impress the stars, the reporters, and, most importantly, Mr. Chewy himself.

"The next point you need to get," the assistant director continues, squaring his shoulders in what I guess is an attempt to convey how crucial it is that we follow the dictums he's declaring, "is that while you are relatively unimportant individually, you *are* important insofar as our needing warm bodies in certain scenes. Sometimes you will make up the members of a large crowd; sometimes you will be near lesser actors; and, occasionally, some of you will be in scenes *right there* with the leads.

"Hear me on this," he goes on. "If you are among those selected for the scenes that necessitate your being near a lead, you are not to in *any* way call attention to yourself or speak to any actor. They are stars; you are extras. I am assuming you understand the difference!"

Lord! I have had fleas biting my butt that annoyed me less than this guy, I think, feeling my short black coat actually bristle. *When I am a star, I am demoting him to assistant to the assistant to the assistant director's assistant!*

Pulling me from my daydream of Matt one day being the butler in my and Mommy's manse is the sudden noisy descent of a helicopter that is landing about thirty yards from our group. Judging by the lightning-quick appearance of about a dozen well-dressed humans hurriedly racing hither, thither and yon and barking commands at one another, you'd think the helicopter must be transporting a king or queen.

Well, as this star-in-the-making is about to learn, it might as well be.

As the human whirlwind continues spinning around me, I look heavenward and watch the whirl of the rotors spin slower and slower as the helicopter begins its descent onto a large X on the lawn beneath it. As it moves closer and closer, I catch a clear view of its famous logo, that beloved-by-all-dogs symbol that makes every one of us smile so brightly, so happily.

Yes, the logo that grows larger and larger as the helicopter continues its descent is probably second only to Kong as the most important name brand on the whole planet. I'm so excited that I quickly hide my lunch box amidst a bunch of nearby props so that I am free to spin in circles fast enough to rival the rotors. Because this is the brand I associate with so much happiness when I see the name on the side of boxes that come to our house. Boxes that contain things not for Mommy but for PD! All the things I love! Toys! Treats! Bully sticks! Even new collars and harnesses feel more fun when they come in that packaging.

Chewy! Chewy, Chewy, Chewy! I sing to myself as I start dancing and reveling and romping and racing about, barking excitedly. Not only am I starring—er, soon to be starring—in a Chewy Productions film, but I also am about to see Mr. Chewy himself! Live and in person! *Wow! Wow! Wow!*

"Hey! You! Black pug dog! Stop goofing around and get out of the landing area!!"

I pause in my prancing and seek the source of this interruption of my preparations to herald the coming of the king. Ah, it's Magpie Matt. Of *course* it is. The assistant director, bringing clean-smell soap to a mud fight. Bringing an appetite suppressant to a kibble convention. Bringing Ralph to my date with my secret fawn girl pug crush. Maybe this guy isn't on a Ralph level of nemesis—*yet*—but *Lord,* is he annoying me.

I freeze mid-spin, not so much out of obeisance to Matt but rather due to the sight before me.

As the helicopter doors open, out jumps not only Mr. Chewy but also both leading men—Horace Heart, who plays the hero in this revenge flick, and Dirk Smirkson, who plays his adversary, the man who done him wrong. The three are joking and laughing and seemingly oblivious to the many sycophants sycophanting all around them. Luggage is collected; drinks are offered; clothing is lint-brushed; the bit of matte face makeup is retouched; "Anything needed?" and "Good flight?" and "this is going to be a great film! Your best yet!" and other rump-kissy comments are blurted. On and on the bustling goes as the production house owner and his two megastars head toward us extras, no doubt on their way to somewhere we lessers are not allowed.

So I have to act fast! No time to lose! *This is my moment to shine!*

Racing to the prop area where I secreted my bone-holding Kong pail, I pop open the box, remove the bone, and . . .

Oooooh, that looks tasty, I think, suddenly lost in daydreams of bone-gnawing pastimes. Maybe I have just a second or two to just get a quick yummy nummy lick or two before carrying out my star-making maneuver. Just one or two chews, just a moment to munch, just a nanosecond to nibble, just . . .

"Not YOU again, black pug!! What on *Earth* are you doing over there?" yells Meddlesome Matt into his megaphone, calling attention to the little dog lying on the lawn just a few yards from where Mr. Chewy and his leads have paused to allow the boss to point out various sets erected both right in our area and a bit farther out, as well as exposing the erenow secret weapon that has been outed.

Move, PD! my brain yells, cutting through the bone-chewing coma to which I nearly succumbed. *Shake a paw! It's make or break time! Bring that bone to the VIPs! Show them your genius and Secure That Star On The Walk!*

With a speed I am sure is unmatched by any pug in history, I hold the bone tightly in my jaws and race like my rump is on fire in the direction of the three men who I know hold my career in their expensively manicured hands. As I reach the now laughing, story-sharing trio, I do a quick tail-chasing spin and launch the bone heavenward.

Score! It lands right where intended! Oh. Um, *sorta* where intended. The aforementioned beautifully manicured hands of Mr. Heart are suddenly a bit, er, wet.

"What *is* this???" a definitely no longer chuckling Mr. Chewy screams, thankfully not at me but at Matt, as both his leads look on, nonplussed. Mr. Smirkson extracts a no doubt pricey handkerchief from his pocket and hands it to his colleague, who starts wiping his PD-saliva-covered hand. "Matt, you better have a darn good reason that the star of my movie is holding a gross, slimy, gooey, drippy dog bone! Lord! There is spittle and slobber getting on his nice suit!! Get some assistants over here with a change of suit, *STAT!*"

Matt looks mortified, but I'll credit him with having some good acting chops of his own. He quickly recovers and points at me, glaring as he does so.

"Mr. Chewy, sir, I'm horrified that one of your"—*smooth going there, Mousey Matt, saying I report to Mr. Chewy and not you*—"backgrounders pulled such a stunt." Matt pauses to glare even more glaringly, were it possible, giving me a stink eye worthy of Ralph's when he sees me marking over a bush he just peed on. "And, heh heh, he's not even a stuntman, of course. He is *nothing.* Just a disposable, toss-away *extra.* We can get rid of him immediately. I assure you, nothing like this will ever happen again on my watch, sir."

"Well, I would *hope* not!" Mr. Chewy blusters, now training his dark glower on me. "That dog is out! *O! U! T! Out!* And Matt, I mean escorted to the parking lot and…"

But his order is cut short thanks to my Hail Mary. *I have to redeem myself!* I think, my mind swirling in panic as I imagine the Hollywood Star I don't even have yet being taken away. *I can't let this happen! I can't get fired before I even start! I can't let this stop my stardom!*

I again start spinning, but this time it's to look in every direction and assess my career-saving options. I toss away one poor idea after another. *No, don't lick Mr. Heart's face. . . . No, don't get in beggy pose before Mr. Chewy. . . . No, don't pee on Matt's shoe. Think, PD, think!*

And then I see it! On an easel near the helicopter—I assume placed there as part of the welcoming pomp and fanfare meant to impress the biggies—is the movie poster. The artwork is beautiful, the fonts are perfect, and the photo retouching is amazing. This poster presents two flawless, handsome men whose fawning public will open their wallets to pay their huge salaries as well as every other cost of this film. This advertisement will help lead this film to unfathomable box office success, bringing in more money than my pug brain can begin to comprehend.

But the only thing about this promotional piece that matters, as far as my own filmdom fate is concerned, are the words at the top:

A Bone to Pick.

A Bone to Pick! A BONE to Pick! A BONE TO PICK!

Channeling the speedy greyhound—a breed which, according to care.com, is the fastest in the world and can run up to forty-five miles per hour—I dash off, no doubt looking like a black blur to the undoubtedly stupefied stars. Moments later I am at the base of the easel, using my hard round noggin to knock the foamboard poster from the horizontal bar on which it rests.

Grabbing the poster in my strong jaws, I race back to Mr. Chewy and lay it at his Ferragamo-clad feet. His expression quickly goes from enraged to enlightened as I tug his pant leg, then press my furry mug over and over and over again on the word on the poster that I thought was the whole point of the film.

Bone.

I am not certain I've made my point until I see a grin break out on his formerly furious face. Even Matt has gone from glare to the slightest upturn of the lip. The two leads, however, still look lost. Thankfully—and surprisingly—it is Matt who does the explaining I can't.

"Oh brother!" he exclaims. "The dopey dog thought the movie was about a bone instead of about revenge! I guess he was trying to impress you, sir, by bringing his own . . . prop? . . . to the set. He's not the brightest bulb, but I have to give him 'props' for creativity.

"Nevertheless, sir, he will be dismissed immediately for this antic. We don't need extras ad-libbing. I made that clear to the group before you arrived, and you can bet this freelancing canine will—"

"Silence!" our employer bellows. "Matt, you will do no such thing! Yes, the little dog misunderstood the film title, but he showed a creative spark nonetheless." Turning his gaze to the gathered gawking audience of extras who have been standing in stunned silence mere feet away, he adds: "Which of you have matched"—here he pauses to read my extra's ID badge—"PD's entrepreneurship? PD's outside-the-box thinking? Hmmm? Anyone? Anyone?"

His speech delivered, he turns his back to re-join his import-ant companions, and they head off toward whatever import-ant place they need to go, leaving me in the hands of Matt, who I fear might be planning on making life difficult for his "entrepreneurial" employee.

But I needn't have fretted.

"And Matt?" the big boss calls over his shoulder. "Find PD a role more befitting his talents. This is no . . . what did you call him? A 'nobody'? A 'nothing'? 'Disposable'?

"Give him a very small part, something with a moment or two of interaction with the principals . . . just something small, mind you."

Mr. Chewy turns around and stares at Matt one last time until the latter slowly nods in acquiescence.

Then this big boss looks at me. "PD, don't mistake this reprieve for approval. Prove to me I am right to keep you in this film. Your attempt to get attention worked. Now you need to work to get the attention of Hollywood.

"And no more shenanigans, or I will have a bone to pick . . . with *you.*"

Chapter Two

BIG THINGS COME IN SMALL . . . ROLES

In the 1980 movie *He Knows You Are Alone,* Tom Hanks had a small role. Four years later he starred in *Forrest Gump.*

In the 1991 movie *Critters,* Leonardo DiCaprio had a small role. Two years later he starred in *This Boy's Life.*

In the 1987 movie *Less Than Zero,* Brad Pitt had a small role. Two years later he starred in *Fight Club.*

In the 2024 movie *A Bone to Pick,* PD the Pug had a small role . . .

Okay, yesterday ended on what could have been a career-ending calamity. But Mr. Chewy, head of a big production house that is producing a big production, recognized true talent when he saw it. And now things once again are going well in my walk toward that Star on the Walk.

I mean, sure, I had a little glitch, but what rising star *doesn't* have a few fumbles as he finds his way to fame and fortune?

Exactly! Lots of today's celebrities had some bumps on that road to stardom, a few booboos, bodges, bumbles, blips. But then they *over*came and *be*came! They became the names you see on those coveted stars on the Walk of Fame.

I mean . . . Sidney Poitier was told by his casting director to stop wasting people's time and become a dishwasher! Katharine Hepburn was called "box office poison"! Lucille Ball was told by her drama instructors that she wouldn't make it in acting! PD the Pug was told by an assistant director that he was a *toss-away, disposable nobody*!

Well, guess what, Matt? I am going to prove you wrong!

Last night, Mommy—knowing my nearly unflappable self-esteem took a hit when Matt tried to get me fired—showed me lots of online tales of stars of today and yesteryear who had rough starts before they joined Hollywood's biggest big shots. She said if they did it, "then my little PD can do it, too!" Then, this morning at eight, Mommy dropped me off at our set and gave me a big Mommy hug before again heading to the roped-off area set aside for cast member family and friends.

So now here I am, about to have my debut acting scene. Not seeing any sign reading "small role actors," I head to the extras' section and present a mask of patience I don't feel inside as I wait to be escorted away from these mere mortals I now deem as beneath an ascending star like myself and placed among others more in my league.

Sadly, it appears that my escort is none other than the person who'd likely prefer setting his hair on fire and putting it out with a hammer over helping the extra who caused his abasement just the day prior. I'm sure Matt is still smarting from the rebuking he suffered. And not just a rebuke, but one from the biggest bigwig of the whole production.

"All right, black pug dog," my charge seethes through gritted teeth, refusing to utter my name like I'm Voldemort or something. "I was told to take you to the studio's restaurant set. Get your lunchbox—and, *Lord,* it'd better have only your actual *lunch* in it today—and come with me."

I grab my Kong pail—yes, containing only the kibble and half a frosted cookie Mommy packed this morning—and I follow Matt, glancing back just long enough to glimpse what I am sure are the envious expressions of my former peers whom I've clearly outgrown on my path to prominence and prestige.

Poor losers, I think, sadly shaking my head over the fact that I am the only one of the dozens and dozens in the extras' crew who will get to laugh with Tom, Brad and Leo over a non-alcoholic beer about all that we share in common regarding our humble starts. Alas, the motley crew behind me will be lucky to get another background stint.

But PD the Pug? Nothing "extra" or "background" about this megastar in the making.

We approach the faux restaurant façade, a neon "Eddie's Eats" sign lighting up the window of its only wall. I assume that behind this wall and its supporting beams are tables, chairs and other diner fixtures to make the set look like an authentic dining establishment. As I stare at the ersatz eatery, I suddenly stop my strut, causing Matt to nearly trip over my small but solid self as I envision myself moments away from sitting at one of those tables. Me! An actual actor about to act with other actual actors!

But wait, I think, *it's even better, were that possible!* Because this launch pad, this blast-off point from which I will begin my meteoric rise to Hollywood icon status, could not be more appropriate. I am a Pug. This is a Restaurant. Pugs love Food. This place will have Food. I mean, they'll have to serve Messrs. Heart and Smirkson food in the scene. And *real* food, not plastic fruit or a rubber chicken, right?

"PD, hold up," Matt commands just as I am about to go inside to see whether the catering crew is preparing food in advance of today's shoot. I figure they might appreciate having a real actor such as myself sample some things and give my opinion. But nope, this party pooper director—ahem, *assistant* director—just has to spoil my plan. He waits until I turn back to face him, then continues, "We need to discuss your part and go over some ground rules."

I grit my strong jaw, making sure not to growl or snort or fart or otherwise show my displeasure to Matt. *Soon enough, I'll be a star,* I remind myself, *and then I can swat this gnat away from this production if not the movie industry in general.* I wag my tail in pretend compliance. *Fake it 'til you make it,* I tell myself, *as any blossoming actor would!*

"First of all, I will remind you that even though Mr. Chewy— for Lord only knows what reason—spared you the axe yesterday, you remain very, *very* low down on the acting totem pole. You are a bit player. Notice the word *bit*, as in tiny, barely noticeable, there but almost unseen.

"And it's that word *unseen* that we producers—we in-charge, important, *seen* people—demand extras and bit players be in every scene, PD. The focus is on the action around you, on the bigger stars, on their expressions and dialogue . . ." Here, this thorn in my flesh narrows his eyes and lowers his bushy brow. ". . . and certainly not on *you*. So don't go pulling any shenanigans like you did yesterday, *dog*."

Remember Mommy's "no bite" rule, I remind myself. *No mauling Matt, no mauling Matt, no mauling Matt . . .*

"Okay, PD, the restaurant scene you're in is short yet pivotal in terms of the movie's revenge theme. By the time our stars meet in the restaurant, there is much tension between them, and it is here that Mr. Heart's character—Jack Galahad—tells Mr. Smirkson's character—Beau Bane—that their temporary truce is over, that Bane should heed the warning to leave town and stop vandalizing his businesses and flirting with his fiancée.

"And when Bane, instead of agreeing to stop his assaults on Galahad's companies and his attempts to woo his bride-to-be, just stares and glares and then snickers . . . *That* is when you and the other diners, in unison, stop eating and gasp.

"That's it, PD. Stop eating and gasp. Got it?"

*What does this assistant—*assistant!*—producer think?* I inwardly fume. *Of course I get it! I am an* actual *actor, Matt! Maybe some* *day you will be an* actual *producer. And not just an Assistant! Assistant! Assistant!*

Finally Magpie Matt stops squawking and we head to the pretend restaurant that I hope has lots of not-pretend food. As we reach the door, we are met by a couple dozen others: small role actors like me, and members of the crew who are scurrying around, presumably to prepare for the shoot.

"PD?" Matt pauses to make sure he has this budding star's full attention. "No monkey business, no fooling around, no nonsense, no bringing your own props! You are to *Sit* and *Stay.* And then *Gasp.*

"I'd hope the first two commands maybe, just *maaaybe,* are something a dog might know so hopefully you can manage the 'gasp' part without any drama. No drama! I'm not kidding around, *dog*!

I reach deep into my acting expressions repertoire and put on my best PD happy face to show Matt I'm on board with his wishes so that we can get on with things. I guess he thinks he has successfully communicated what I am to do in the scene and finally we enter the makeshift building, which does look just like a real eatery, what with its tables, chairs and even an easel-mounted menu board featuring the day's specials and daily lunch offerings.

As I stare at the listed items—Sandwiches! Soups! Pasta! Hamburgers! Chicken! Even steaks!!—my tummy rumbles just thinking about the possibility of numerous takes and, hopefully, retakes and a plate that is piled with yum over and over and over and . . .

"PD! Stop licking the floor by the menu board and get over here!" Matt barks from his position next to one of the dozen or so tables in this faux diner. Reluctantly I turn from the food listings and give him my attention, knowing that the sooner the shoot begins, the sooner I hopefully will be eating.

"Okay, you will be a patron here at this table near the bar. Why the production team wanted you here of all places is a complete mystery to me, because it is right next to table one, the table where our leads will be seated, the table where all the dialogue happens, the table where the main action occurs. It's where our leads drink their scotch, have their tense moment and then end their truce. It's one of the most important scenes in the movie and . . ."

Matt pauses and raises his eyes to where the ceiling would be were this a real restaurant and takes a deep breath, perhaps trying to get centered or calm or something. Which, were he an *actor* like *me*, he could easily *do*. I am just about to offer free acting advice when he again focuses on me. "Lord, from a nearly canned extra to having the best seat in the scene. Clearly an oversight!"

Anxious to show off my acting skills to Messrs. Heart and Smirkson, I rush to my waiting chair, knowing that the sooner all us actors *(actors! not extras!)* get situated, the sooner I will be *sitting* and *staying* and *gasping* my way right into my next movie role. A bigger role. Maybe even the role that lands me my first Oscar.

Can't you just see it? Me? On the stage standing before the podium on the big night of the Academy Awards? Accepting my first Oscar for Best Actor? Accepting the statuette from the male presenter and getting a soft head pat from his female colleague? Taking my speech from where it's rolled around my collar and . . .

"PD!" Matt says in what I guess would be called a very loud stage whisper. "Get *off* the table, quit barking into your fork like it was a microphone, and sit down!"

Chastised in front of my acting chums is not the way I saw this going, but, being a professional, I roll with it, quietly chuckling in a way I hope conveys this was part of the scene setup or some such. I sit at my table—its "Table Two" plastic sign causing me to excitedly turn to look at the "Table One" brass sign denoting the seating site of the leads, whose immediate surrounding area is roped off, discouraging lookie-loos from getting too close.

Of course some of us—we more important acting colleagues—are assigned to be neighbors with the biggies. So I of course am a big enough deal to be closer than others, and . . .

"PD!! Get out from underneath the leads' table and get back over here right *now!*" Matt yells into a bullhorn he has just plucked from the hands of one of the assistants who is rushing around, leading other actors to their assigned places. I assume his goal in going from metal megaphone to a device that allows the electronic amplification of his voice is to up my mortification in front of the now-filling-up room. And he proves my assumption true seconds later as he stands right next to my empty seat and whaps it with the hard device. "*You!* Black pug dog! Get. Over. Here. Right. *Now!* Any more goofing around and I'm calling Mr. Chewy."

And how did tattling work out for you yesterday, Meddler Matt? I think while reluctantly obeying.

"PD, somehow you not only have the best table as far as proximity to the stars but also somehow get it all to yourself," Matt says, shaking his head and making the sort of face Mommy makes when something confounds her, like when I chewed through my new bed whose ad claimed it was indestructible.

As the catering crew sets out dining plates and starts filling them with the food we all will dine on during the shoot—some tables get hamburgers and fries, others chicken breasts and roasted veggies, still others spaghetti and meatballs—I obey Matt and climb up onto my chair. I try and focus on him, but I can't help peeking around to see who is getting which dish. *Please give me a hamburger!* I think. *No, wait, chicken. No, no, spaghetti! With extra meatballs! No, hold it . . .*

"PD! Pay attention!" Matt growls. "Again, your whole performance centers on the *gasp*. When Beau Bane—Mr. Smirkson's character—reacts to the warning from Jack Galahad—Mr. Heart's character—with a snicker, all of you stop eating, jerk your heads up in unison . . . and *gasp*. Got it?"

Okay. Jerk and gasp. Jerk and gasp. Jerk and gasp, I think while watching a catering crew member place what looks like a very juicy medium-well hamburger on my plate. Another member follows, dropping a pile of french fries on my plate beside the burger. The aromas are nearly hypnotizing, and for a moment I am daydreaming of that time Mommy walked away from a plate with a just-cooked burger she had left on the ottoman, and the next thing I knew my little stout self had leapt up and . . .

"Um, sir—er, dog—I don't think you are supposed to be up on your table," whispers one of the serving staff. "And please don't sneak fries before filming starts, or that man over there is going to get upset."

That "man over there" is none other than Meddlesome Matt, who is giving me the stink eye. I reluctantly climb down and get back in my chair, telling myself it will be mere moments until I am sampling my yummy-looking meal. Yes, it is only ten in the morning, but every hour is lunch hour when you're on Pug Standard Time.

By now, all the other actors have taken their places, so eleven of the twelve tables are occupied. Only the seats awaiting Messrs. Heart and Smirkson remain empty. As Matt noted, I am the only one without a dining companion; I decide that must mean I am a bigger deal than my fellow bit players. I mean, the closest seat to the leads *and* no one sharing my table? Clearly they want to audience to focus more on me, me, me!

But right now every eye in the room is focused on the two men who've just entered this mock dining establishment. Other than when I catch my own reflection, I've never been in such proximity to greatness. These are real stars! These are the ones I aspire to be! Well, I mean still *me*, but like *them!*

Sit up, PD! I command myself, channeling Miss Sophia and imagining myself on my best behavior. As the two men take their places at table one, I bear my snaggliest snaggletooth grin. *Hey! I think Mr. Smirkson winked at me!! Or was he practicing squinting evilly at Mr. Heart?* No matter; I will just choose to believe I was noticed by one of the biggies. And, being as we're restaurant neighbors, I just know I will get a chance to impress them somehow.

"All right, everyone," Matt says with a lilt that certainly was not in his speech tone when yipping at me just moments before, "let's get ready for the shoot. I'll will be here as backup, but I'd like to introduce the woman who will oversee this scene shoot. Everyone, meet Deborah, the executive director of *A Bone to Pick.*"

Seconds later, in walks a short-legged but fast-moving heavy-set woman carrying a clapperboard.

"Greetings, all, I'm Deborah," she says as Matt annoyingly plants his annoying self next to me, no doubt to make sure I don't do anything he deems acting up. "I am so excited Mr. Chewy hired me to direct this fabulous film. And it's wonderful to again work with our stars! I've led three films featuring Mr. Heart and one—the Chewy Productions film—that featured Mr. Smirkson. No doubt you all remember *Bad Day At The Dog Park*—won the coveted Tail Wagger Award and was talked about for an Oscar. I am hoping this film will be Mr. Chewy's first Academy Award."

Geesh, nothing like putting on the pressure, Lady, I think, imagining Mommy and me at the awards ceremony. *Now I know I need to wow everyone and really stand out in this scene!*

"Okay," our executive director continues, "when I clap the board and shout 'Action!' you all start dining. Just focus on your meals. And while you aren't loudly speaking, you are of course moving your heads and smiling and enjoying your outing.

"As Matt mentioned, our leads will perform their parts as you dine, and when you hear Mr. Smirkson's character snicker, you will cease eating and *gasp*. Again, when Mr. Smirkson's character, Mr. Bane, snickers, all of you in unison *stop eating* and *gasp*. It's important that the gasp is one collective sound. Everyone clear?"

We all nod as Deborah picks up the clapperboard and goes to the front of the room near the bar. Matt finally leaves my side, but not before whispering in my button ear.

"Dog? You do anything to embarrass me in front of Deborah, and you are done as an actor. Done. Done. *Done!*" Matt threat-whispers before plastering on a fake smile and heading to Director Debbie's side.

Refusing to let him get to me, I join the other actors in focusing on Deborah, who now has her clapperboard raised and is moments away from initiating what will be my first step, if you will, toward the Walk. Toward my own star on that Hollywood tourist destination. Toward . . .

"And, ACTION!"

As the stars and the rest of us dig in, I can sense one camera panning around the room while the second is fixed on table one. Deborah is staring at Messrs. Heart and Smirkson, while Matt seems overly focused on yours truly. Probably willing for me to mess up. But no, Matt, I am a brilliant actor who already has mastered the essence of this scene: eating. All I need to do now is eat and pay close attention to the leads, then give a gasp to beat all gasps.

Oh. My. Stars. This hamburger is *so* scrumptious, juicy, savorous, flavorful! These fries are so greasy, fatty, salty, crispy! My mouth and belly are experiencing so many different kinds of happy—the pleasure center of my pug brain is experiencing so many different kinds of pleasure—that it takes all my willpower to tune in to the dialogue that has just begun at the table next to me.

                    GALAHAD
        (sitting erect, both hands flat
     on the tabletop, looking intently)
    Look, Bane, I've been patient. I've
    shown restraint. I've allowed your
    efforts to ruin my businesses to go
    unpunished. I've turned the other
    cheek when you dared to wink at my
    fair bride-to-be, but you've shown
    no remorse.
    So now . . . I have a BONE to pick
    with you.

                    BANE
            (expression smug,
            head shaking slowly)
    Pitiful, Galahad, you're just . . .

    BANE snickers.

    THE DINERS stop eating and . . .

Near silence fills the restaurant. Then a collective GASP. Except . . .

Munch! Munch! Munch . . . !!!

Heart, Smirkson, every actor in the room, every member of the crew—including a dumbfounded Deborah and a crimson-hued, *very* Mad Matt—jerk their heads my way as the last bite of burger sends some savory succulence down my chin, some oily yum that my lightning-quick tongue laps into my parted maw.

"Cut!" yells Deborah before snapping her perplexed face over to Matt, who looks like he'd rather be anywhere but here.

"PD!" he bellows into his bullhorn from his place at the bar. "PD, how difficult *is* this? I said when Bain *snickers* you *stop eating* and *GASP!* Looking first at the nonplussed stars and then addressing the room at large, he adds, "Everyone, I'm very sorry for this..."—here he glares at me—"bit player's obvious misunderstanding of the scene. Um PD, heh heh, let's remember: at the snicker, stop eating and GASP."

Thankfully this slightly nicer version of Mean Matt has taken over for the moment.

"Okay, Matt, thank you," Deborah says, pushing down the bullhorn and turning to the catering crew. "Please refill the plates, and let's try again."

Refill the plates? A reprieve and more food? Yippee!

But my happiness is short-lived, and the next twenty minutes are a bit of a blur:

"ACTION!"

". . . (Snicker)"

(Nearly collective) "GASP!"

(Except:)

"Slurp! Slurp! Sluuuuuuuuuuuuuurp!"

(Bullhorn-enhanced:) "PD!!! Stop sucking in that long piece of pasta!!!"

And then:

"ACTION!"

". . . (Snicker)"

(Nearly collective) "GASP!"

(Except:)

"Chew! Chew! Cheeeeeeeew! GULP! Chew! Chew! Cheeeeeeeew!"

(Bullhorn-enhanced:) "PD!!! Spit out that chicken breast right now! Are you gasping-impaired??"

A displeased Deborah again knocks the bullhorn out of her way and then glares at me while addressing the room. "Everyone, go and get some air. We will do another take in fifteen minutes."

"And PD?" she adds, narrowing her stare. "I heard about yesterday's shenanigans and Mr. Chewy's graciously giving you a second chance. Let's not make him regret that kindness. This is my Oscar shot, PD. Don't cause me to have a bone to pick with *You.*

Chapter Three

TO BE OR NOT TO BE (SACKED)

Albert Einstein said, "Failure is success in progress."

Robert F. Kennedy said, "Only those who dare to fail greatly can ever achieve greatly."

And Thomas Edison said, "I have not failed. I've just found ten thousand ways that won't work."

Well precisely, Al! Spot on, Bobby! Nailed it, Tom! If these purveyors of wisdom claim booboos can lead to triumph, victory, mastery, well who am I to argue?

These sage thoughts rattle around my pug brain as I stroll around the studio grounds during the break from this morning's shoot. While it may be true that I could have paid a tad more attention to the "stop eating" part of Matt's directive, my not following his law to the letter wasn't *that* big a deal, right? I mean, Deborah didn't can me. She must see my potential. Clearly she has the wisdom to overlook this fledgling's little fumble.

As I walk along, I give thanks to the gods of generosity that allowed us to take a sandwich with us as we left the restaurant set. Because, I have to say, despite having three meals, I am still a little hungry. Acting takes it out of you, you know.

Now that I know my chances of stardom remain intact, I again can feel secure about my chances of one day breathing the rarefied air drawn into the lungs of only the luminariest of Hollywood luminaries. So without a worry in the world, I decide to use the rest of this short break (*how did my sandwich disappear in the first five minutes?*) strolling down the section that is lined with the trailers that house the big shots featured in our film. I look at the stars on the doors and read the names that soon will appear on screen when our movie is released to the theaters and online.

Just as I am smilingly daydreaming of one day decorating PD's double-wide, my happy dream suddenly turns to what feels like the scariest nightmare I've ever experienced. I stand there numb, uncomprehending, dazed, unnerved, dumbstruck. I must look catatonic to any onlooker as I stare slack-jawed at the trailer in front of me.

What?!! Am I hallucinating? Did someone put some PCP in PD's PBJ? Does that trailer door's star say Ralph the Dog?? Oh, No it does Not! No! No! No!!

Forget that rarified air; I can barely breathe at all. I haven't been this agitated, this flustered, this unnerved since that giant black mastiff at the dog park licked my whole face in one big drippy lick and I thought I was drowning.

But no, I reassure myself. *No, clearly I'm in some altered state of consciousness from what had to have been a drugged sandwich. Because if that mangy mutt ends up on this movie's marquee, I will Strike! I will Picket! I will Demonstrate! I will Boycott! I will . . . I will . . .*

I pace back and forth in front of the white mobile home bearing the name of my nemesis (see *No, YOU Sit! PD the Pug's Manual for How to Train Your Human* and *Working Like A . . . Dog! PD the Pug in Corporate America*), trying to think up more ways those in Hollywood fight for their rights. Then I calm my anxious mind by deciding there is no way that that mongrel is a movie star so there must be some *other* dog named Ralph in the cast. *Yes, that's it! How silly of me to think that hound of hell would even be an* extra, *let alone . . .*

But before I can finish that hopeful thought, the trailer's white aluminum door swings out, knocking me off my pug paws and sending me sprawling onto the pavement. As I regain my footing and try to regain my dignity, I come face to face with the ghastliest, vilest, wretchedest, scuzziest sight imaginable. Well, imaginable for me, anyway.

Ralph. Ralph the Dog. The vilest of villains, the foulest of foes. The object of all my loathing. The only dog I truly detest.

And this scamp, this scoundrel, this scumbag certainly is no screen star! *No!* The only top billing I will allow this scalawag is top billing in my daily ploys to defeat him. A dog never had a bigger rival than I have in this dirtbag. Any reader of my previous books is well-versed in his *unsuccessful* attempts to mark over my pees, woo my secret fawn girl pug crush, ruin my landscaping work (in chapter three of *Working Like A . . . Dog!*) and his many other failed efforts to one-up your hero, PD.

There's no way I'm going to let this scummy scamp one-up me here.

Our eyes meet—did he just pull a "Bane" and *snicker?* At *me?*—and in my mind's eye I suddenly am transported from this movie set to every real-life set at which we've encountered one another or even just known the other was there. Foul memories of this foulest of fleabags flood my mind: the rank smell of his pee before I again mark over it; the disgust of being doused with his drippings the time he shook his rain-soaked muddy mess of fur as we passed on that walkie; the havoc he wreaked at my aforementioned landscaping job; and, by far the greatest offense, his sniffing around my secret fawn girl pug crush.

Channeling Alexander the Great—considered the greatest warrior of all time—I prepare my mind and body for battle, for a dogfight to end all dogfights. I thrust out my broad barrel chest, jut my jaw, and face the foul fiend.

Ralph stands before me, trying his sorry best to appear intimating. Annoyingly, he pauses to look back at the big white plastic star on his door, then turns back to me, snickering yet again as he does a condescending head shake.

But I refuse to take the bait. I know that before this shoot is over I'll get higher billing than this film-star fraudster, this drama dud ever dreamed of.

The aforementioned Alexander the Great once said, "I am not afraid of an army of lions led by a sheep; I am afraid of an army of sheep led by a lion." So I, PD the Lion, need not fear the sheepdog in front of me. I will vanquish him just like King Alexander vanquished his enemies in each of the many battles he fought and won. I am PD the Great! This mutt in front me is Ralph the Nothing!

Just as I am preparing to pounce, I sense movement in my periphery. Deciding it's likely a restaurant scene actor or crew member who's on break like me, I tune it out and focus on the netherworldly ne'er-do-well before me. I think of high jump record-holder Javier Sotomayor of Salamanca, Spain—who in 1993 leapt nearly eight and a half feet—and tell myself that merely leaping onto Ralph's head should be a piece of cake.

I start a mental countdown-to-pounce. *Five . . . four . . . three . . .* Suddenly the movement I noted moments ago feels like it's getting closer. I turn from Ralph to see who or what is encroaching on my mini battlefield, and I imagine King Alexander's ire at being interrupted just as he was about to clobber his foe. But wait—*what?*

". . . And *action,* Ralph! Good stance! Great paw placement! Perfect facial expression! Now give us a snarl! And now another snicker! Good. . . . *Good* !"

What is this?? One of the movie's cameramen is *filming* us! And he's making Ralph seem like the good guy to my villain! I won't have this! I am Alexander! He is Memnon of Rhodes (considered by many accounts to be King Alex's biggest foe)! And you can bet that the photog will capture the scene *correctly*, because . . .

Whomp!! Out of nowhere, a heavy mass of fur and bones has flattened your hero, PD. I feel like my lungs are two deflated bags, and they're filling with stinky Ralph stench as I struggle to shove him off of me. My whole pug self is smushed under this demon dog who not only seems to have bought into the *lie* that he is a bigger star than me, but also seems to believe he has subdued me! And on *film* to boot!

But no! I will not be abashed by this greatest of my rivals! And certainly not on camera with the possibility of it one day soon being viewed by my Mommy and my secret fawn girl pug—the former at the movies, the latter when it comes to the small screen on which she'll maybe watch it with her own human Mommy. I won't let this mortification occur at all—and I certainly won't let it be witnessed by *A Bone To Pick*'s audience!

With that thought in mind, I gather enough air into my flattened lungs, gather enough physical strength, gather enough positive thoughts to push revolting Ralph off of me. Before he can react, I steel myself, bare my snaggletooth and its teeth brethren and . . . *Ram!* I barrel into him, thoroughly enjoying the shocked look on his face.

But just when I think I have the upper paw, just as I am about to make my move to maul this mutt, I freeze in pre-strike pose as that voice again blares into my delicate pug ears.

"And CUT!" yells the director. "Ralph, don't fret," she says in an annoyingly fawning tone. "We'll edit out the part after you subdue this black pug dog. Don't worry at all. The scene will cut to you drinking non-alcoholic dog beer with Mr. Heart's character, laughing with him over his defeat of Mr. Smirkson's character and your drubbing of this dog, this . . . Mr. . . . I'm sorry, *who* are you?"

Merriam-Webster's dictionary defines *mortification* as "a sense of humiliation and shame caused by something that wounds one's pride or self-respect." Britannica dictionary defines it as causing one "to feel very embarrassed and foolish." And vocabulary.com says you are mortified "when you're so ashamed or embarrassed that you wish you could just shrivel up and die."

Pretty much.

Who am I? I fume, my outrage slowly supplanting my embarrassment. *Who am I?? I am PD the Pug! Film-star-to-be! The first pug to very soon have a star on the Hollywood Walk of Fame! The only thing Ralph deserves is a star on the walk of shame!! Because he brings shame to all dogs just by existing and . . .*

But just as I am gathering back my self-esteem and preparing to squash Ralph like the bug he is, and doing so in such a choreographed way that this guy no doubt will see who's the better dog star, the photographer pats that miscreant on the head before reaching into his pocket for a Nature's Path bully stick—my favorite brand!—and putting it at Ralph's feet. My biggest enemy does his final bit of acting: doing another snicker (!), taking the coveted bully stick in his maw, ascending the trailer's three steps and slamming the door so hard that his Ralph the Dog star nearly falls off its hook.

The last time I felt this demeaned from feeling one-downed was that time at Bark and Boarding's Sunday Funday when that little bitty dwarf Yorkshire terrier pushed me off the toy bench I was lying on and all the other dogs *snickered.* Just like Ralph *snickered!!* And just like *that* time of mortification, when, *doggone it,* I got my seat back (okay, it was five minutes before Sunday Funday ended and ninety percent of the dogs were gone, but *still*), I am going to vindicate myself here! But this time, not only will I get the upper hand against the reeking Ralph, but I'll also get my star—both on my own trailer and very soon thereafter on the Walk of Fame!

Then everyone in Tinseltown will know my name! Never again will someone look at me and say, "Who are you?"

I'm ready to get back to the restaurant set and show Deborah, Matt and the leads how great acting is done! My own trailer! My own entourage! My own PD PR team! Stardom is one great scene away!

Nothing can stop me now . . .

Chapter Four

THIS DOG'S ON FIRE

During a boathouse scene in *The Amityville Horror,* police arrived to tell the production crew that a dead body had been found floating nearby.

While filming the Sermon on the Mount scene in *The Passion of the Christ,* actor Jim Caviezel was struck by lightning.

A majority of *The Titanic* cast and crew were poisoned with PCP-spiked clam chowder and had to be rushed to the hospital at one in the morning.

The point of these factoids from buzzfeed.com? Things could be a lot worse! I mean, comparatively, my little setbacks—the ill-received gooey bone I presented to Mr. Chewy and the leads; my failure to pause eating when Bane snickered; Ralph seemingly whomping my behind (and on *film* to boot)—are big nothing burgers. I mean, no dead bodies or lightning strikes or everyone strung out on PCP, right?

Exactly! Fame and fortune remain my forecast!

Okay, I'll admit that yesterday ended better than I expected it to. After my *very* marginal misunderstanding of the "stop eating" command, miraculously all was forgiven! Director Deborah clearly recognized that sometimes even the most talented of actors has a misstep. I mean, starsinsider.com tells us that in the 1988 film *Rain Man*, there's a scene where Tom Cruise and Dustin Hoffman are crammed together in a phone booth and Hoffman did an unplanned fart! He just ad-libbed it! And they left it in the movie! And then Dustin Hoffman won the Best Actor Oscar!

Do I have to spell it out for you? Great actors like *me* commonly have a few farts on their way to super stardom!

Here's what happened. When I got back to the set following that humiliating encounter with Ralph, I felt like a dead pug walking. I'd messed up the restaurant shoot, I'd upset Director Deborah and maybe the movie's stars, I'd come across—due to that ill-timed cut while I was the literal under-dog (as in *under* my archrival's body)—as losing a battle to *Ralph*. Ralph of all dogs! But would-be executioner Deborah gave me a stay! And not a "Stay!" like from Miss Sophia, my trainer, but a stay like being able to stay in the movie!

As I and the other actors and crew gathered around our leader, Deborah explained that the talented chief videographer was able to edit out my little background noises, making it sound as if everyone had gasped. That means no one—not Mommy, not my secret fawn girl pug crush, not Aunt Jackie, nor any other audience member watching *A Bone to Pick* on the big screen—will ever know that PD pulled a boner.

"Chewy Productions' top-notch editors are well versed in audio source separation, allowing them to isolate an undesired signal component and remove it without affecting the rest of the audio track," Deborah explained. "That means we needn't reshoot the scene and you all can take the afternoon off while the crew finishes final touches on the set for tomorrow's filming."

"In other words, little screwup pug dog," Matt had snarled in his annoying stage whisper inches from my head, "your insubordinate, wayward, defiant, rebellious *chewing* and *munching* and *slurping* could be eliminated. And thanks to modern technology, your absentminded, oblivious, inattentive boneheadedness will not cause us to have to redo that whole scene! Which is too bad, because maybe then you'd have been fired like you deserve!"

(PD note: I guess I should mention here that Deborah sorta didn't have a choice on whether to can me or not. I overheard her mentioning to Matt that Bane looked my way when he read the menu board, "and so that little food-scarfing, scene-sabotaging, unteachable trainwreck of a dog can't be totally edited out. Unfortunately!")

But things got even better! Deborah then got a call that someone who was supposed to have a tiny part in the *next* scene had the flu. And since there was no time to do more auditions and keep to the shooting schedule and . . . PD the Pug was ready and able . . . well, Voilà! (Matt might have argued with her, but Deborah needed a warm body—and what's warmer than a furry pug?)

So yesterday was just an overall spectacular day! I got to stay in the movie *and* I got to go home early! Mommy did her usual over-the-top Team PD cheerleading, treating the onlookers to lots of hollers and hurrahs and hosannahs and other celebratory noises when she greeted me at the front of the spectator section and carried me all the way to the SUV yelling "PD the Star! PD the Star!" Lord almighty, the woman was even wearing an "I Have A Movie Star Son" T-shirt with a black pug on it that she had made on Etsy. I was super embarrassed and was wishing she'd tone it down already!

Except, wait . . . okay, that's a fib. Because, c'mon—I *am* PD the Star! And if this second reprieve doesn't prove that, then I don't know what does.

So now it's the next morning and as I exit Mommy's SUV and start hoofing my way to where the other minor players are gathering. I can't stifle a bit of a smug pug smile. *Too bad for you, Matt!* I think to myself. *PD the Pug is still in this movie! And I'm going to do such a great job in the next scene that when the film comes out, the Oscar humans will have to create a whole new category called "Best Bit Player." And then, on Oscar night when I'm holding my statuette and giving my speech, I'll thank everyone who worked on this film except You because . . .*

"Hey! Black pug dog! Are you planning to join us over here, or are you just going to keep barking into that stick and prancing around and being the court jester you are?" Matt snarls angrily into the megaphone that I know he is using solely to amplify his voice to embarrass me. "Because *some* of us"—here he pauses to do a slow panning with the megaphone across the many actors and crew members standing around him—have a movie to make!"

As I trot over to join the group, I glance toward the spectator area and see Mommy standing in the front row, today sporting a "PD has a Bone To Pick with you!" Etsy-created top that features another black pug, this one holding aloft a bone à la Luke Skywalker taking on Darth Vader with his lightsaber. She blows me a kiss, and I nearly chase my tail and woof in appreciation, but, seeing as I already have one strike against me this morning, I think better of it and sit my rump down.

"Oh goodie. The star-in-his-own-fuzzy-brain has decided to join us commoners," Matt says sarcastically, pausing to do a squinty-eyed glare at me before finally lowering his megaphone "Sorry for the late start, but now that *everyone* is here"—Lord, another gloomy glower—"we can begin."

Matt picks up a clipboard with several papers attached. "Today's shoot resumes where yesterday's left off. As you know, the previous scene ended with Bane threatening Hart. While our editors fixed the PD-caused audio problem"— yep, third grouchy grimace—"the crew did some close-shot filming of our stars to finish the scene without the diners needed in the background. The restaurant part ended with Bane rising after the crowd's gasp quieted and he began his exit. Galahad then rose as well and said, 'Not so fast, Bane. I said I have a bone to pick with you. I have had enough of your vile actions, your diabolical attempts to cause harm to my business and personal life . . . Outside, Bane! Now!'"

Matt goes on to explain that today we will be out in the town square, where Hart and Bane will have a tense confrontation. As he continues his speech, I take in the newly constructed set around us. Old-timey façades of buildings from yesteryear line a mock street. One side features a saloon, a general store, a candy store, and a butcher shop. Across the way are the restaurant, a post office, a firehouse, and City Hall. But on this day, the script says, the shops and offices will be emptied out, and all the employees and patrons—played by heartthrob PD the Pug and the other bit players—will be in their respective doorways or in the street, watching as the two human time bombs threaten to detonate before them.

Matt stands at the entrance to the faux butcher shop, filling me and the other bit players in on what the next scene includes and what is expected of us. While Galahad and Bane face off, he says, we townsfolk will be staring at the brewing battle before us, looking frightened with jaws agape and eyes agog. We are to stand stock still, doing nothing to take the audience's focus away from the stars.

Lord, then the lecture from this nagging gnat begins.

"In case any of you"—Geesh! fourth pause, fourth stink eye—"need reminding, you are *background* players. That means you are *not* the focus of the scene. It *also* means that you follow Deborah and my direction to the *letter*, without *improvisation*, without *extemporization*, without *ad-libbing*. That said, your role in this scene is threefold:

"One: come through your assigned door and either stay in the doorway or rush to the street near your building.

"Two: Look frightened and react as anyone observing a tense powder-keg situation would.

"Three: When the tussle begins, look terrified, turn to your neighbors, and then turn back to the fight in the street."

Okay, I think, *easy peasy. All I do is exit the door and then either stay or walkie to the street. And then look fraidy face. No problem! I've got this!*

Adding to my confidence is the approach of Director Deborah, who—*Thank you, God*—replaces Matt at the door to the makeshift meat market and holds up a sheet of paper. I feel so much better knowing Matt won't be in charge of this shoot by himself. I, um, don't think I'm his favorite cast member . . .

"Okay, gang, listen up," Deborah begins. "This morning, my assistants wrote up this list, randomly assigning each of you to the building you will exit and stand in front of to watch the confrontation between our stars. Some of you will be closer, some farther away, but all of you are an important part of this scene. We want the audience to sense that this part of the town is a busy business district and that you all are the proprietors, the employees, the common folk."

We all nod along, but c'mon, there's nothing "common" about PD the Pug, superstar-to-be! But she can apologize to me on Oscar night. For now, I just need to concentrate on being the best crowd member. And on not messing up again. Which, of course, I won't. I mean, how can you screw up just standing there? *I've got this, I've got this, I've got this, I've . . .*

"PD?"

I am so focused on my little PD pep talk that it takes a beat for me to snap my head in my director's direction.

"Would you *please* stop pacing and barking to yourself and pay attention?!"

Chastised, I force myself not to hang my round head in shame and instead stand tall—well, tall for me—and wag my tail in compliance. Out of the corner of my eye, I spy Matt smirking at me and holding up a finger.

"That's one," he mouths silently.

Big deal, Matt, I think. *You're not the one I need to dazzle. I am going to do such a great job in this scene that Deborah will tell Mr. Chewy how sagacious, how discerning, how percipient he was to have given me not just another chance after my slobbery bone boner, but a bigger role!*

Thankfully, although I'm still fuming inside, I have stopped pacing, so Deborah is none the wiser about my plan to blow her away with my acting talent. I put on my best 'good dog' expression—eyes all a-googly, round head tilted to the side in curiosity—and I strive to concentrate on her words as she explains the coming scene.

"Mr. Hart's character, Galahad, will follow Mr. Smirkson's character, Bane, out of the restaurant and grab him by the upper arm. Their dialogue will start off calmly, then escalate. Next, Mr. Bane will draw his sidearm, shoot a round into the air, and warn Mr. Galahad, saying something about 'next time it's your head.' You *then* exit your buildings and look both excited and frightened as you watch the brewing battle."

I grin my snaggletoothed grin and do some excited tongue-out panting to show Director Deb my complete comprehension.

"Okay, here are your assignments, alphabetically by name. Martha Abbey, City Hall; Karl Buxley, the general store; Darla Edwards, the butcher shop, then go into the street a few feet outside your building . . ."

I zone out, knowing it will be a while until Deborah gets to P. Then I glance around and notice that all the other players seem to be hyper-focused on our director. I take a moment to ponder how I might stand out a bit from the actors around me.

For example, there is a fire hydrant by the firehouse. Doing a nice long weewee would cause me to draw eyes, but only stink ones. If I get assigned to exit the candy store, I could have Mommy run to the store and grab a giant lollipop I could be exaggeratedly licking. But that might cause me to focus more on the sucker than the fight. If the faux butcher shop has faux cleavers, I could enter the brawl and help Galahad! Oh, wait. PD plus cleaver plus no opposable thumbs might be a bad plan. *Think, PD—think!*

But it seems I will have to stow the star-making strategizing for now.

". . . Marie Peterson, candy store; PD the Pug, firehouse, then go into the street; Steven Roberts . . ."

Deborah finishes the list and everyone now has a building assignment. About two-thirds of the three dozen or so of us are to stay in our doorways; the remaining third are to step out into the street, closer to the action. I am giddy to not only get to be a pretend firefighter but also to *once again* be right in the thick of things! Think of all the close-up screen time I'm getting! First the restaurant table by the stars, and now this! I'm so excited that I have to force myself not to run to the spectator section and lick my beaming, waving, photo-shooting Mommy all over her smiley face!

But guess who's about to bring a stinky cat to the dog party?

"Deborah, excuse me, but is this a good idea?" Meddling Matt has edged closer to my boss and is shaking his head and acting all fakey, like he has her and the film's interests at heart. But I know better, and seconds later I am proven right.

"I mean," he says, the firehouse is *right next to* the restaurant. Do you think it's a good idea for PD to not only come out of the *nearest* building to the restaurant but also to stand nearest to the *stars* in the *street?*"

Channeling Charles Bronson, Steve McQueen, Bruce Lee, John Wayne and every movie tough guy I can think of, I square my pug withers—dog shoulders, for readers not up on canine anatomy—and try to appear unbothered. But despite my tough-dog stance, inside I'm feeling insecure, threatened, uncertain. This is the most nervous I've been since that time I smelled my secret fawn girl pug crush's scent on that bush and thought she was right next to me!

Matt continues his hatchet job. "I'm sorry, but this little dog has already upset our stars twice! And I heard he had a scuffle with poor, innocent Ralph the Dog during the break! The dog has dogged up everything he touches. I already am envisioning ways he will bungle his"—here Matt pauses to give me that trademark glower—"*insignificant* role in a way that *significantly* and *negatively* affects this important scene! Let's either leave PD in the firehouse doorway or better yet have him off somewhere fighting a fire!"

Deborah, my judge and jury, shakes her head. "PD and the other bit actors were randomly assigned these tiny background roles. They stand and observe. There is nothing to mess up. Please leave the directing decisions to me and go get Brenda."

As Matt scurries off to get this Brenda person, I imagine him as a scolded dog with his tail between his legs. Overall, this is a great day in my acting career! I am super anxious to hear the clap of the clapperboard and for Deborah to yell "Action!" and for PD to begin showing these other bit players how it's done!

"Hi, I'm Brenda!" says a petite, very oddly dressed twenty-something woman. She is pushing a rolling clothing rack laden with dozens of period costumes that look like they're from Mommy's great-great-grandparents' closet. Brenda's purple hair, orange-sequined dress, purple leggings and thigh-high gold boots seem less bizarre when she explains she is Chewy Productions' costume designer.

"Now," she happily exclaims, as if this is good news, "we've chosen great outfits for each of you for this scene! You all are going to look just perfect for your roles! So if you will just line up and give me your name, I'll give you your costume."

(PD note: My second book, No, YOU Sit! *PD the Pug's Manual for How To Train Your Human, includes an entire chapter about my disdain for wearing clothing. It's both wonderful and awful that I am a very popular little pug on Instagram—wonderful because it's fun to have so many Insta PD Pals, but sometimes awful because many of the posts feature me in one of the more than a hundred costumes Mommy has dressed me in for the enjoyment of thousands of humans and the mortification of one Mr. PD the Pug. In fact, if you'd like to see my giant wardrobe closet, check out the video Mommy posted on March 28, 2022, at instagram.com/pd.the.pug!)*

Fifteen minutes later, I am attired in full firefighter's gear: helmet, gloves, heavy coat, boots, the works. I even have a long hose looped around my large pug head. I somehow feel both manly and ridiculous. But when I look around, I feel like I got off easy. Candy store proprietor Marie is turned out in bright green coveralls and carrying a gingerbread house; city hall "judge" Martha is wearing a powdered wig, a black robe, and a lace collar and is holding a gavel; Darla, the butcher, is sporting a white apron complete with faux blood stains; and each of the other background cast members is dressed in some equally silly manner matching his or her profession.

I turn and *of course* spy Mommy with her iPhone raised high, camera in Burst mode, taking picture after picture no doubt to post online tomorrow. I decide to make her smile by putting a gloved forepaw up in the air in a wave to my Instagram fans. I'm about to do a little jump-rope with the hose for a video when Deborah says it's time for our scene.

"Okay, everyone, get inside your buildings," she instructs. "There is a speaker behind each door, and you will be told when to come out, so pay attention. When I give you the cue, either stand in your doorway or come out to the street, per your assignment."

Moments later I am excitedly standing behind the ersatz firehouse's door, eager to come out and show Deborah what a great thespian I am. As I wait for the moment to exit my building, I am racking my pug brain for ways I can stand *out* and not just stand *there*. I have to shine! I have to impress! What to *do*, what to *do*, what to *do* . . .

Snapping me out of my PD-star-making strategizing is a soft voice emanating from the speaker:

"All background players, prepare to come out of your doors in three . . . two . . . one . . . Exit!"

We all come racing out of our respective doorways; I emulate my fellow actors looking both curious and alarmed at the two men staring one another down in the street, and back to one another.

"Bane?" Galahad says menacingly, "I didn't want it to come to this, didn't want to have to harm you, but I have no choice other than to pick that bone I have to pick with you. This has gone far enough!"

We all look on tremulously as Galahad's rival stares at him contemptuously. Bane shakes his head and scoffs. And then pulls a cigarette and lighter from his shirt pocket, making clear that he thinks he's in charge of when the anticipated fight will begin. The townspeople look on all aquiver, waiting to see if these human volcanoes are going to erupt.

Well, all the townspeople save one.

There I was, minding PD's Ps and Qs, doing what I thought was a superb acting job—watching the tense action in the street with the appropriate facial expressions while simultaneously still figuring how I can stand out without upsetting the higher-ups. I was just thinking that my Deborah-eye-catching act could maybe be related to my firefighter role when . . .

FLICK!! goes Bane's lighter!

Talk about opportunity knocking! Or flicking, at least!

Fire!! Fire!! An actual firefighting emergency! Just steps away from my very own firehouse! I imagine the pseudo townspeople seeking my very real services as they chant, *Help us, PD the Firepug! Help us, PD the Firepug! Put out the fire, PD the Firepug!* I can't let them down! I *won't* let them down!

Realizing that my hose has no connection to a water source, I know that saving the surrounding structures from total conflagration is down to yours truly putting out that flicked flame with just my firefighting skills, gleaned from, um, years of training in the, um, firefighting academy. Which means I can either spit a bunch of times or . . .

POUNCE!

I hear a muffled *grunt!* as I pin baddie Bane to the ground and knock the wind from his lungs. As I stand on him in my tiny fire boots, I give thanks for the production team's wisdom in putting me nearest to the movie's leads. Since I was just a few feet from this firebug, I could quickly act to save the day. Feeling quite the hero, I perk up my little ears, anxiously and joyfully anticipating the psalms of praise from the town's proprietors whose buildings and very livelihood I have saved.

But what I hear next doesn't sound much like the *Hallelujah Chorus.*

"Security!!"

"Matt!"

"Ralph the Dog!"

Wait! Stop! Let me explain! As about ten personal assistants to Mr. Smirkson rush to the star's side, shove me off him and then slowly help him to his feet, I scramble my brain for good excuses to get me out of the mess I've unwittingly caused. I mean, the *fault*—assuming there *is* any, which I surely do *not!*—actually lies with the production crew who named me town firefighter! *I am PD the Firepug! My job is to put out fires! Bane lit a fire. Ergo*—duh!—*PD the Firepug was putting out the fire!*

But if the action around me is any indication, it doesn't appear my plea is working. Deborah's glare rivals the angriest death stare Bane ever gave Galahad; the man alongside her dressed not in costume but in a very real "Security" uniform doesn't look too appreciative either; and the foul mound of fur alongside *him*—yep, Ralph—is pretending to be all-Mr.-star-on-the-trailer actor dog as he snarls and foams and looks at me all fakey menacingly.

The slow clap I hear behind me is not the kind I fantasized about getting when presented with the now unlikely Oscar. Slowly turning so as not to get tased or pounced on, I see the horriblest human on Earth has joined the growing group; and he is holding up two fingers and snidely winking.

"And that's two, *dog*," he doesn't bother mouthing it or even whispering. Matt wants the whole "town" to know how much trouble I'm in. He nods his head and smirks at me as he stands aside to let the big security man in to the group around me which now includes Matt, Ralph, Deborah, Brenda and . . . oh no . . . even worried-looking Mommy (the only one here not angry). *Well,* I try and console myself, *at least it can't get any worse.*

But I'm wrong. I'm just so, *so* wrong.

Twack twack twack . . .

I look skyward and see a sight more anxiety-provoking than the time my auto-shipped Nature's Path bully sticks were delayed and I was all out for like two whole days. More scary than the time the lights went out and Mommy watched a dog movie in the dark on her iPad and I kept hearing a menacing growl inside my own house. More tummy-upsetting that the time I thought that toy pizza slice toy was real and I bit into it and swallowed the squeaker.

As the Chewy helicopter makes its slow descent onto the pawprint-shaped helipad, I try and remember the prayers of petition I've heard Mommy utter when she is worried about something and seeks divine help. Sadly, the only prayer I bothered to memorize was grace, because it results in the praying one getting food.

I glance behind me at the gang of glowerers (only Mommy is still looking at me hopefully) and note that Messrs. Heart and Smirkson are now standing off to the side, staring at me while whispering to one another. Smirkson actually guffaws as Heart says something in his ear. I'm guessing it's something about my pending demise and about my slobbery bone presentation being only the first of multiple bone-headed moves.

Several assistants rush to the helicopter door as it swings open; two of them reach out to take each of Mr. Chewy's arms to assist him as he steps down to the ground. I can't discern his facial expression, mostly because he is not looking my way but rather at the two big stars he is striding toward. The three huddle and I imagine my Hollywood Star being peed on by Ralph as the most important humans in my life right now (well, after Mommy, I mean) hold what looks like a mini conference, a meeting on my fate. I feel like I'm in more trouble than that time Mommy was having a dinner party and I did a poopie on the dining room carpet. I hang my head in anticipation of hearing not only "PD, you're fired!" but also "and here is Mr. Smirkson's indictment against you so get ready for prison!!"

So to say the least, I am not expecting what I hear next.

The laughter starts as a couple of quiet chuckles, and grows to giggles, chortles, snorts, and finally belly-clutching roars as the men in charge of not only my movie star destiny but maybe my legal one finally turn in my direction. I expect that seeing the dog that caused today's mess will be enough to sober them up, but to my continued surprise they only laugh all the harder, wiping their tearing eyes. Finally Mr. Chewy straightens up and addresses me.

"PD? Let me get this straight. Am I to understand that you . . ." Here he and his stars break into another round of guffaws . . ." Am I to understand that you pretended you were a real firefighter and leapt on Dirk when he flicked his lighter?" He wipes his eyes again. "I just . . . PD . . . you're something else."

Matt, obviously thinking he finally is rid of me, jumps into the conversation.

"Yes, Mr. Chewy, to the amazement of Deborah, myself, the other bit players and unfortunately, even one of our top stars, this inept, incompetent, irredeemable walking fiasco actually thought he was a real firefighter and that he was— wait for it!—putting out a fire! Fred is here to escort him off the property and I can have legal here in ten minutes if Mr. Smirkson wants to file an assault charge."

I raise up on my hind legs, placing my forepaws together for Fred the security guard to slap his cuffs on guilty little me. I am so focused on getting arrested that I don't realize three bodies have come to my side. And so the slap I do get is doubly unexpected.

Mr. Smirkson gives me the kind of buddy back clap you give someone with whom you share a good joke. Instead of the angry glare I am expecting, he and his colleagues are grinning ear to ear.

"Matt?" The only glare in this moment is directed at our assistant (*Assistant!* Sorry, can't resist) director. "Take a breath." Turning back to me, he says, "You know, PD, Heart was just reminding us of the time he did this film about chimney sweeps and he was so into character that he wouldn't bathe for a week and he was so covered in soot that one night his wife mistook him for a burglar and whapped him over the head with a frying pan and he was laid up for a month. It was hysterical!

"PD, if you can immerse yourself that thoroughly in a character, then the sky is the limit as far as the roles you can play. Frankly, it took Heart and me years to attain the level of acting skill you've shown us in just a few days."

I note wide grins on the faces of Messrs. Heart and Chewy as this grantor of my reprieve turns to our director.

"Deborah, have the editors cut out the lighter part and just go from Galahad saying "this has gone far enough" to our stare-down and then to the next lines. I'm anti-smoking, personally, and I don't mind that being cut out, so we can thank PD for keeping children from thinking cigarettes are cool, too."

The whole group, save pouty-face Matt, is laughing now. Mommy is the happiest with me I've seen her since Aunt Tammy gave her a Nordies gift card "from PD" last Christmas.

Matt turns to stomp off but trips over my firehose in what has to feel like the afternoon's final indignity.

But it's not.

"PD, I have to agree with Dirk," the boss of all bosses chimes in with the sweetest melody I could hear. "Deborah, let's finish up this scene and then get everyone ready for the big fight scene in the town arena. I want PD to be front and center amongst the spectators. He clearly truly cares about the success of Chewy Productions. I reward good behavior."

Matt cringes as he adds: "Good dog, PD. *Very* good dog."

Chapter Five

THE PD METHOD

For his role as blind blues musician Ray Charles in the film *Ray*, actor Jamie Foxx had his eyes glued shut for fourteen hours a day so he could wear prosthetic eyelids that were modeled to look like Charles'. (hollywoodreporter.com)

For his role as Hugh Glass in the film *The Revenant*, vegan actor Leonardo DiCaprio ate raw bison. He also camped in the wilderness in below-freezing temperatures, risking hypothermia, and he slept inside animal carcasses. (hollywoodreporter.com)

For his role as Lt. Col. Frank Slade in the film *Scent of a Woman*, actor Al Pacino attended a school for the blind and reportedly asked for advice from vision-impaired individuals. He lived his daily life as if he were blind and told crew on set to treat him as if he were a blind person. (hollywoodreporter.com)

For his role as heroic firefighter PD the Firepug in the film *A Bone to Pick,* actor PD the Pug . . .

Method acting—or "The Method," if you will—was developed by Russian actor and director Konstantin Stanislavski. It describes the performance by an actor who is fully immersed in the part he or she is playing. Unlike classical acting, which is mainly action-based, method acting draws in the *emotions,* allowing the actor to virtually *inhabit* the character.

Great method actors—like, say, *me* in my firefighter role— put our whole physical, mental and emotional selves into the creation of a character. That is what Mr. Smirkson and his co-star and our big boss all saw in my stupendous performance when I *became* the firepug I was playing and, um, saved the whole town from going up in flames.

And let's not forget how method actor PD was also one with his character in the restaurant. This dining dog *became* the hungry patron, absolutely *craving* the hamburger, the chicken, the spaghetti. His character was *starving;* three full meals were needed to fully satiate him. Clearly it was a convincing portrayal, leading the higher-ups to assign me to another opportunity to exhibit my acting abilities. And, again, PD's perfect performance wowed everyone.

And that is why, on this morning after the face-off between Galahad and Bane and my saving the town from total conflagration, Mommy and I once again are walking from the parking lot—why I don't yet have a reserved parking spot is beyond me—to the spectator area where I'm to await today's assignment. I think Mommy wants to come to the set with me, but only *actors* are allowed, *Mother.*

Leaving my cheerleader-wannabe Mommy to her twirling, swirling, whirling and other gyrations of support (today her T-shirt reads "Ask Me About My Movie Star Son"), I head to an annoyed-looking Matt, who's staring at his clipboard. As his eyes travel from papers to pug, he has an expression like that man at the park had that time I yanked myself free of Mommy and jumped on the bench next to him and stuck my face in the scrummy yummy melty cheese of his nachos.

"Argh, you're like a bad penny!" says Matt, slapping the side of his head. "*Why?* Why can't you get *fired?*! Why do you *keep coming back?* Why do you *haunt* me?"

He holds his clipboard aloft, and for just a moment I fear it's about to land on my thick pug head. I squeeze my googlies tightly shut and brace for a fairly decent headache but when I'm still pain-free several seconds later, I risk a peek. Instead of looking my way, Matt is watching the approach of his superior, who seems surprisingly upbeat, even showing a bit of pep in her step.

"Matt! I've just come from a meeting at Chewy headquarters," Deborah begins. "I have mostly good news. First, our crack team of editors were again able to do an edit using some extra footage so that the shot goes from Bane's scoff to Galahad's close-up look of total fury. We took the time they were editing to shoot a short scene in the home of Galahad's mother-in-law-to-be, Naomi, who is hiding her daughter,

Catherine, away from the lecherous Bane. Then we can just jump seamlessly to the final showdown in the town arena."

Then Director Deborah turns and looks sadly at me before turning back to Matt. "The bad news is that the actor Mr. Chewy sees as the most up-and-coming, the likeliest to be going places, the most blossoming of all the other bit players—PD the Pug—had to be largely cut from the scene.

I can tell you the boss is not happy about that, but he said as long as PD is in the arena scene, all is fine."

Matt holds up his hand, obviously wanting to make some silly objection about, ahem, "up-and-coming" *moi*. Luckily for me, Deborah is distractedly pacing, intensely focused on her star in the making and ignoring Matt the Gnat.

"I just need to decide what role he'll play in the arena scene," she ponders aloud as she picks up the pace of her pacing. I mean . . . is PD a mere bystander, or is he protecting the townsfolk from the catastrophic calamity about to crash in on them?? Is he given a line or two?"

Deborah ping-pongs her head from Matt to me. "The big point is that Mr. Chewy has been twice impressed by PD—first when he brought the bone prop to our stars, and then yesterday when he—okay, in his own mind, but still—saved the town from an inferno. And the boss made clear to me that PD needs a top bit player role in this next scene. I'll go over the script and see who I can swap out."

The reactions of Matt and me could not be more completely contrary. Your hero PD's barrel chest is puffed out so far I worry for a moment about exploding and sending hundreds of pug pieces into the stratosphere. Meanwhile, Matt is so still you'd think he was a statue. He looks numb, dumbstruck, colorless, spiritless, listless.

"Matt! Snap to!" Deborah shouts while waving her hands in front of her underling's glazed-over eyes. "Get everyone to the arena and text me when the set is ready. We need to be rolling in an hour." Turning to giddy me, she adds, "PD? Go to the craft services tent by the stars' trailers and get your free lunch. I need you fueled up and ready to impress both me and your colleagues!"

And by "colleagues," I think as I dogtrot to the chuck wagon, she of course means Messrs. Heart and Smirkson—not the riffraff, the refuse, the rabble, those unwashed bit players and extras whom I have far outshined! I mean, of everyone here, I am the only one attracting the eye of the big boss. My acting career is on the fast track, and . . .

As I debate whether to invite Mr. Chewy to the ceremony when my Hollywood Walk Star is unveiled, my sunny mood suddenly darkens. Blocking my path into the cafeteria tent is a sight that causes me to almost—I'm a pug, folks; nothing can *totally* spoil it—lose my appetite.

"And . . .*Yes!* Work it! And now look over your right shoulder! *Yes!* And now the left! *Perfect!* And now go from "sit" to "roll over." Love it! *Love it!*"

Am I *hallucinating?* Is that a *photographer* shooting shots of *Ralph??* And does that shutterbug's shirt actually say *Celeb Dog Magazine???*

Though I'm holding onto hope that the scene before me is a mirage—that I merely am experiencing low blood sugar due to a lack of lunch—I can't help but feel uncharacteristically clumsy, unsteady, as I wobble forward for a closer look. I am so focused on this nightmare-come-to-life that I don't notice the photographer's tripod until my furry little foot meets one of its legs. I shuffle and stumble, trying unsuccessfully to regain my footing, and . . .

Smack!!!

My round head has landed smack dab in the center of a plate of dog biscuits—here, I assume, for the photog to offer to that wretched Ralph as rewards for good poses. I can't help myself from scarfing a couple of the bigger ones before I push myself up from the treat dish. I look around frantically for an escape route, but I am caught out.

"Hey! You! Black pug!" Sadly, the now crimson-faced cameraman is blocking my progress, standing dead-center between me and our cafeteria. My belly's growling is overridden only by my desire to get away before my enemy gets a good look at me. I figure I've got about ten seconds to dart into the makeshift lunchroom before Ralph unfreezes from the (fake! pretend!) big-shot pose he is holding for this paparazzo.

Alas, the Fates are not with your pal PD. Ralph is startled out of his *Vogue* moment as the photographer continues screaming and screeching at me. The snippy picture-snapper seems to get more infuriated as he lectures, angry about both my "interrupting his artistic process" and—I can hardly bear to share this—my "inconveniencing Ralph the Dog, who now has to be here longer, which might impact his keeping to his very busy and important schedule!"

The only thing more mortifying than the cameraman's words is the response to all this by that despicable dog he is lauding. As Ralph peers around the shutter man to see what is causing the ruckus, he actually pretends to *not know* me! Like we haven't had a *years-long* Hatfield/McCoy relationship! Like he doesn't *recognize* me as the dog that always—*always!*—out-marks him on every bush and tree! Like he doesn't *recall* how my secret fawn girl pug crush is *mine, mine, mine!*

Embarrassment and fury battle in my temporal lobe for control of my emotions. And then my stomach rumbles, usurping them both. I search about for a path to the diner's door. Just as I am trying to squeeze through the still-yelling artiste's alternately stomping legs, I come face to shin with the one person I was hoping to avoid on my so-called lunch break.

"Matt!" the photographer yells, "thank goodness you're here! As you know, I am with *Celeb Dog Magazine,* here to get shots for this month's cover story on the top dog in *A Bone to Pick.*" Here he pauses to give me a squinty-eyed scowl before turning back to my second biggest enemy on this Earth.

"There I was, working hard to get perfect images of perfect little Ralph the Dog when this *other* dog"—another glower my way—"comes stumble-bumbling into our obviously private area and starts traipsing and tripping and tumbling all over tarnation!"

Matt might as well be at a tennis match the way his head is snapping from me to magazine man and back again. He looks Heavenward, as if beseeching God Himself to help him through this moment, before addressing us.

"Look, I'm really sorry for the actions of this pug dog," he says, addressing the photographer while shooting daggers at me. "But I can't say I am surprised." He goes on to recount what he considers my other "offenses"—which were *not* offenses, as they each led to a promotion!—as the camera bug's eyes continue bugging out.

"*Just get him out of here!*" the photog roars. "At this point, I am just hoping Ralph the Dog is gracious enough not to reschedule. His agent gave our publication only an hour for this shoot, and this clumsy mutt has set us back several minutes, as well as affected my artistic focus!"

Wait. Agent? Ralph has an *agent*?

Sometimes when I'm curled up next to Mommy on the couch, she gently shakes me to wake me from mewling in my sleep. She always says something about "you were having a nightmare" and "everything's okay." Well, this business of Ralph getting famous is a nightmare I can't shake off, and *nothing* is okay! I haven't felt this flabbergasted since I learned my beloved bully sticks are made from bull wienies.

My state of stupefaction is overcome only by my fear of further incurring this so-called *artiste's* wrath. I turn to scurry off toward the buffet, but just as I go to finally make my getaway, Matt apparently feels the need to give me one more snippet of snark.

"Hey, PD," he says quietly through gritted teeth. I halt and turn to face him. He does a smug smirk and holds up three fingers. "And *that's* three."

I know in human talk, you get three chances. I guess that's it, then. I guess my short-lived stroll toward that coveted Hollywood Star is over. I guess . . .

"Matt? *What* is going on here? *Why* don't I have a text on the status of the arena set? *Why* is PD getting hassled by you instead of getting some sustenance as I directed? *Why* is there a photographer here doing a shoot I didn't know about and didn't approve? I *told* you Mr. Chewy wants PD to have a noted role in the fight scene. I *told* you he needs to be ready. Instead, I find him here—unfed, unprepared, and made to feel unwelcome by you and this . . . *who* are you?"

I can barely contain my snaggletooth grin as Deborah— standing feet away with a styrofoam container that I assume contains her to-go order from our dinette—lays into Mean Matt and camera bug. What she says next is such fantastic news that I fear my rollercoaster emotions will cause my little pug heart to give out:

Good thing: Deborah tells Matt to personally escort me to the chuck wagon and, on her authority, to go to the head of the line so I am, as she puts it, "fueled up and full of good acting energy."

Great thing: Matt is now the one getting the figurative finger. Deborah tells him he gets two more chances to show her why she hired him as her second-in-command in the directorship hierarchy.

Stupendous thing: Deborah tells me that she has met with the scriptwriter, and that my arena role will be to actually hand Galahad his pistol for his duel with Bane. Wow! Wow! Wow! My third scene with the leads! (Um, hopefully three's a charm and this time the scene will make it into the film!)

Funniest-thing-I-ever-heard thing: Turns out Deborah is not the only one who wasn't told about this mysterious photo shoot. Turns out it was Ralph's Mommy who called this paparazzo—and paid an obscene rate—to *hopefully, maybe* get her precious Ralph featured in *Celeb Dog Magazine.* When Deborah reached her on the phone, his Mommy admitted as much and also to paying the trailer company for Ralph's trailer rental! My eyes water from guffawing as I learn both the photo shoot and the rental have been canceled.

As Matt and I go skipping off—okay, I am the only one skipping—I happily realize that my pug appetite has returned, following an unfamiliar absence while I dealt with so much stress. I further realize that I haven't eaten in hours and find myself hoping they have some of that spaghetti left from the restaurant scene, because I liked those meatballs a lot! They were nice and big and spiced just right and . . . But no, no, wait! I also really liked the hamburger, because it was just so juicy and . . . But, oooh, what about the chicken? I loved the chicken because it was so yummy nummy in my tummy and . . .

"PD? Would you please stop drooling and staring off into space?" snaps Matt. "I have thirty minutes to get you fed and to the arena. Move it!"

For the first time, I am more than happy to follow Mr. *Assistant Director's* directive. I mean, I'll follow just about anyone's directive if there is food on the other side of obedience. As I follow him to the head of the grub line, my empty pug belly grumbles and I take in so many pleasant smells I feel lightheaded.

True to her word, Deborah apparently has let the staff know I am authorized to cut to the front of the line, because no one gives me the stink eye. Annoyingly, Matt doesn't wait for me to peruse the specials board; he just orders for us both.

"Two orders fried chicken, please," he says to the waitperson in a *far* nicer tone than he has ever used with me. He adds, "And I'll have a Coke—and a bottled water and a bowl for the dog." As the man turns to get our meals, Matt changes his fakey-face smile to his normal nasty expression and addresses me.

"PD," he says, narrowing his eyes, "you have ten minutes to eat your chicken, and then we are going to the arena and you are going to do as I direct and you are not going to cause any more problems for me. Do. You. Understand??"

Well, everything but the "ten minutes" part, I think as I wag my tail in pretend acquiescence. I mean, who needs ten minutes to eat anything, let alone greasy, paw-licking-good fried chicken? I'll struggle to make it last two rotations of the wall clock's second hand.

I follow Matt to a table in the center of the room and jump up on a chair as he sets our plates down and pours my bottled water into a bowl. Just as I am about to savor my first bite of crispy, oily bird meat, I hear the word *pug* mentioned a couple tables away. Hard as it is for this food-focused dog, I pause with the fried food against my flews—dog lips, for any uneducated humans reading this—finally putting the drumstick down so I can concentrate on the conversation.

"Do you really think that's him, Smirkson? That pioneering pug? I can't think of his name . . ."

"Yeah, Heart! That's him! That's, um, PD! That funny little slobber-bone bearer! And let's not forget town-saving firepug!"

By now the film's big stars are holding their sides and clapping each other's backs and guffawing, drawing stares from the other diners who are looking about for this pug the big shots are talking about. I risk a direct look at the table—the only one with a white tablecloth and China and real silverware—and luck out by catching the eye of Mr. Heart. His bright white grin lights up his whole face as he elbows his giggling friend and points at me.

"Great," my dining companion grimaces at me. "Now you're not only the laughingstock of the movie but you're making a fool of yourself—again—in the presence of the leads! Now stop staring and eat your meal. We have to leave in a couple minutes."

Oops . . . looks like we might be late.

"Hey, uh, Mark? Maurice? Mike?" We look up to see that Heart and Smirkson have come up to our table and are addressing my semi-boss but mostly looking at me. "Mind if we say a quick howdy to PD?"

"Um, sure, guys, great to see you again. As you know, I'm *Matt*, the assistant director of this great film, and let me be the first to say . . ."

But the movie idols have tuned him out. "Yeah, thanks, Maurice," Smirkson says as he and Heart turn to me, their faces beaming. Smirkson says, "PD! Buddy! Mr. Chewy says you're going to be in the big fight scene with us. That's great!"

Heart leans in and pats my head, saying, "You remind me of me when I was just getting started in Hollywood. I did whatever it took to stand out—and just look at me now. Keep up the good work, little pal!"

As the stars turn to leave, Heart winks at me and says, "See you on set, PD! Can't wait to see how you wow us this time!"

Smirkson adds, "See ya, PD! See ya, Maurice!"

As they walk off, I taunt the Grim Reaper by slowly raising my eyes. Maurice—er, Matt's—expression has quickly gone from fakey-smiley to bafflement to barely contained rage.

"PD, I am *telling* you," he spits at me through teeth so gritted I worry one of them might crack, "if you do anything—*anything!*—in the arena scene that embarrasses me or gets me in trouble, you will regret it! You are still just a nobody bit player, and you'd be wise to remember that!"

Actually, Matt, I think with a snagglegrin on my proud pug face as we head to the scene of the big battle, *you'd be wise to remember that I'm the "buddy" and you're the duddy nobody!*

And you know what else I think? I think Matt won't get an invite to my Hollywood Star ceremony. Not a chance.

Chapter Six

BRINGING A PD TO A GUNFIGHT

In the masterpiece movie *Gladiator*, Cicero is the servant and friend of the Roman general Maximus Meridius—the latter played by Hollywood heartthrob Russell Crowe. There is a scene in the film where Maximus orders Cicero to fetch his sword . . .

Cicero is played by Thomas Flanagan, who has appeared in more than forty films and more than twenty television shows.

In the masterpiece movie *A Bone to Pick,* Black Dog is the servant and friend of the gallant Galahad—the latter played by Hollywood heartthrob Horace Heart. There is a scene in the film where Galahad orders Black Dog to fetch his pistol . . .

Black Dog is played by PD the Pug, who soon will appear in more than . . .

As I approach the very real-looking arena where the big showdown between Galahad and Bane is to take place, I am working hard on this odd trait humans strive for called "humility." It's something silly to do with trying to come across as unpresuming, unpretentious, unostentatious. Like you're not exceptional, extraordinary, excellent. Like you're just as dull, dreary, and drab as those other ho-hum hum-drummers out there.

Lord, I thought pretending I'm starving to death and fake-fainting when Great Auntie Sheila puts away the dog bakery cookies was a challenge!

And let's face it, it's hard not to be a bit swellheaded when you're as, well, swell as me. I mean, it's one thing for biased Mommy to tell me I'm stupendous and tremendous, but it's quite another for a big director like Deborah, or a big production house owner like Mr. Chewy or a big movie star like Mr. Hart or Mr. Smirkson to make you feel as phenomenal as I feel right now.

Which makes it all the more imperative that I rein it in. Soon, I will have my Hollywood Star and my Oscar and my Emmy—and, maybe if I take bass lessons from Uncle Robbie, who plays the bass in a band in New Orleans, my Grammy. Then the contracts for celebrity endorsements will stream in, and that's when I can stop masquerading as a modest little mutt. But today, I have to focus on no foul-ups. I am moments away from again wowing my colleagues, and if I have to pretend I'm a bit less astonishing than I am to make sure my name is on this film's credits roll, then so be it.

The arena set looks so realistic! Despite this film's small-town feel, the oval space in front of me looks sort of like a small Roman amphitheater. I summon the ghost of Cicero and imagine that Galahad has (of course) summoned the ghost of Maximus as we *become* the servant and his gladiator and prepare to take on Bane.

And I'm so ready to get to acting! My pug belly is nicely sated from both my own fried chicken and the extra thigh that was sitting untouched on the plate of a glaring Matt who finally *bammed!* it on my plate when I would't stop staring and whining. And then I was given five minutes to go potty before Matt walked me here and told me to wait for Brenda to come get me all costumed up.

As I wait for our costume director to arrive, I glance over at the spectator area, where friends and family are allowed to sit and watch. Today Mommy is wearing a ball cap featuring a black pug dressed like Superman. Her T-shirt reads *PD is Super Duper!* in a yellow and red shield shaped like Superman's iconic *S* logo. I want to say it's a bit much, but, well, I *am* pretty super.

Several minutes later, the rest of the bit players have arrived and the crew is getting them situated. Some are seated in the rows of the arena's bleachers; some are scattered here and there on the ground near where I assume the action is to take place. In the front row are the actresses playing Galahad's fiancée, Catherine, and her mother, Naomi.

There is a lot of excitement in the air, and I have to say I am probably the most excited of everyone here! Because I have *such* a prominent role! I'm the sidekick, the chum, the confidante, the compadre. I have to think *A Bone to Pick* will go on to become the best buddy film of all time, because it has the best film buddy—*ME!*

I'm so busy daydreaming about a sequel for this film—maybe Galahad and me as a modern-day *Turner and Hooch,* except even better and funnier!—that I don't realize Brenda is standing in front of me. And that's saying a lot, as this woman is hard to miss. Today she is clashingly clad in a black corset over a long red crinoline skirt and green combat boots. As I look from the boots to her still-purple hair, I'm reminded of my costume in chapter four of my third book, *Working Like A . . . Dog!* when I performed at a children's party with a family of clowns.

"Hi, PD!" chirps Brenda as she thrusts out what looks like a gunslinger costume. I'm reminded of Clint Eastwood in *The Good, The Bad and The Ugly,* which is lauded by many as the greatest gunslinger Western of all time. My costume includes black pants with belt and holster, a Western style shirt, a brown vest, a brown derby hat, and little black boots. I feel so cool just looking at it that I almost give a thumbs-up in Mommy's direction, but I refrain, knowing she would just take it as permission to keep dressing me up for Instagram.

Brenda rushes off to clothe my fellow actors, leaving me and my no-opposable-thumbs self to figure how to get my costume on. Thankfully, Miss Marie, my candy store pal from the town square shoot, sees me struggling and hurries over—well, hurries as fast as one can when clad in vintage white lace pantaloons under a red hoop-skirted dress. She puts down her humongous prop lollipop and gets me suited up.

"Looking good, PD!" Marie says, admiring her work. "I'd better get to the set. I get to stand kinda close to the big showdown. But"—here, she leans in and whispers discreetly—"wow, PD! Everyone is talking about *your* big part! No more firefighter pug for you! No! Now you're right there in the thick of the action: handing Galahad a pistol! "And I get to say I *dressed* you! I'm going to go tell *everybody* !"

Marie scurries off to tell the other bit players she has been in the presence of greatness. Truthfully, I'm super impressed with me, too. Even more so—were that possible—now that I know Marie and the other minor actors all recognize me as the one among us who just keeps exceeding and excelling, getting promotion after promotion as I work my way toward that Star on the Walk.

I'm feeling so good right now that nothing can dim my gleaming snagglesmile, not even the sight of both Matt *and* Ralph—the latter on a leash, now that his star ranking has been lowered to stink-stank-stunk—heading my way. I take a deep breath like Mommy doing Pilates and tell myself that there's nothing either of these wannabes—Ralph the wannabe star; Matt the wannabe *real, not assistant* director—can do or say to foul my mood.

Ugh. Except . . .

"PD, Deborah wants Ralph the Dog to sit in and observe you today," Matt says, unsuccessfully trying to hide his mirth over my having to deal with this disgrace to all dogs in my orbit and taking mental notes on how he can follow me along the road to renown, down the street to a Star. Matt continues: "Deborah wants you to show Ralph how a dog can go from extra to bit player to"—he pauses to cough and do an over-the-top eye roll—"*top* bit player by impressing the higher-ups."

I repress my fury, mostly because I don't want to give Matt and Mr. mange mutt the satisfaction of seeing me lose my cool. And let's be honest: I can't. Because here comes my superior, the woman whose opinion I actually care about. Although I've managed to get this far despite my *teeny,* almost *unnoticeable* booboos, I do know that she might not tolerate another PD miscue on her movie set.

"Oh, PD, good!" she exclaims. "You already know I want Ralph the Dog to shadow you a bit on this shoot. You've wowed Mr. Chewy, the stars and me, so I was thinking that . . ."

Suddenly a loud fart goes off, interrupting Deborah's train of thought. I look over at the obvious culprit, my understudy, whose action clearly is a statement of displeasure. He *pffffts* out another, then follows it with an "it wasn't me" innocent dog look before nodding toward Matt. The latter, looking very red-faced (whether from anger or embarrassment over getting the fart blame, I can't say), glares at Ralph and then opens his mouth to protest, but Deborah cuts him off.

"Matt? Go get the stars from their trailers and bring them to the set. Get everyone in place. Text me when everyone is ready. I'll bring these two." Turning back to me, she continues: "Anyway, PD, don't worry; Ralph won't be underfoot. I just want him to watch you practice before the shoot and maybe learn a bit from you. Then I can determine if he is going to be in the scene at all."

I risk a glance at my enemy. Ralph looks more chagrined than the time we got in that big peeing battle after he snuck onto the grounds of the estate I was helping to landscape in my third book, *Working Like A . . . Dog!* He was one of the reasons I got fired *then*; I'll be doggoned if he is going to get me fired *now*.

Deborah begins to lay out the scene we are to shoot and catches us up—*me, not us! Me, the only actor here!*—on where things are in the overall plot of the movie. After all, I am only privy to what has happened in the scenes I've (sorta) been in. Deborah wants me to get a feel for where things stand with Galahad and Bane. I guess a rising star like me needs to know this because . . .

"PD? Pay attention. I said you need to know why you are in this arena scene . . ."

A snort causes her to stop mid-thought.

"Ralph, stop snickering. I don't even know if you have a chance of appearing in this film at all. So zip it . . ."

I try and keep still but can't help but make a face at Ralph.

"PD, stop sticking your tongue out! Both. Of. You. Stop."

When Deborah is satisfied that we are paying attention to her and not about to get in a real-life dogfight, she starts to tell us the plot thus far:

"The theme of *A Bone to Pick* is good versus evil and getting even with someone who wrongs you. Galahad, of course, represents good, and Bane is the bad guy." Deborah explains that in the early scenes, before your fave movie-icon-to-be PD appeared in the restaurant scene, Bane had nearly succeeded in a hostile takeover of Galahad's business and had then dared to try and "take over" the romancing of Galahad's fiancée, Catherine. The threat issued in the restaurant scene escalated to the demand for a duel in the arena. Other filler scenes have introduced Catherine's loving and protective mother, Naomi; featured Galahad hard at work at his successful business; depicted Bane at home plotting nefarious deeds against his rival; and flashed back in time to when the leads were teenage rivals in school.

Deborah continues: "So the movie audience now is going to see the big climax: the duel. Everything has led up to this most intense, exciting, nail-biting moment, and you, PD"—here she holds my gaze—"have a very important—even if very short—part to play."

The only thing better than being such a V.I.PD is knowing my biggest enemy has fallen so very far: from having a (*fake! bought!*) star on a (*rented!*) trailer to having to be my understudy. He's giving it the ol' college try, but there is no way he can completely mask his mortification. This cur is the Bane to my Galahad, and I one day will totally vanquish him, just as I know Galahad will one day totally vanquish his own rival.

"Would you two please stop circling one another and pay attention?" Deborah implores. "Okay, PD, Brenda is getting a prop pistol to put in your holster. You will follow just behind Galahad as the two of you walk from off-camera to the center of the arena grounds. Bane and a stand-in will come in from the other side. The stand-in is a placeholder during the practice take while I decide if Ralph the Dog can handle that part. If not, then the stand-in will stay in the scene."

Holding Ralph's stare, Deborah lowers her voice an octave. "Ralph? After all the nonsense you and your mother have pulled, you are lucky I am even *considering* you for this tiny role. Bane's sidekick is barely in the scene; the back of his head might be all we see of him. But this would at least put you in the film. So pay close, respectful, attention to PD here, and I'll make my decision based on your actions."

Yeah, Ralph, I think, giving him the side eye. *Respect the star dog!*

As Deborah leads us to one side, just off camera, I see Matt arriving with Brenda and the leads. The latter each have three assistants who are walking backwards while applying the stars' final touches of makeup and dusting off their duel-worthy wear (Wrangler jeans, a tailored Western pearl snap shirt, and cowboy boots for Galahad; corduroy pants, brown suede shirt, and combat boots for his sworn enemy).

Brenda peels off from the group and heads my way, reaching into a large knapsack as she walks.

"Here you go, PD!" she sings, handing me a very real-looking prop gun. "Don't shoot yourself in the paw! Ha-ha!"

Brenda bounces off, leaving me feeling quite macho as I look at the faux weapon in my paw. I decide now's as good a time as any to start impressing everyone. I want to show Deborah how wise she was to give me this big role. So, channeling Old West gun spinners, I try to spin the pistol before plunking it in my holster. Alas, I don't have experience in gun twirling, and I end up just sorta tossing the gun in the air and watching it land . . . on Mr. Smirkson's foot.

"Good grief, what was *that*?" he howls as he limps a couple feet away from the heavy prop and looks about for the culprit. "Good thing I have on sturdy boots! Who *did* that?"

Four stink eyes focus on me from under Deborah's and Matt's glowering brows.

Matt speaks first. "Sir, let me *again* apologize for PD the Pug. He apparently was practicing a 'gun-spinning' move decidedly *not* in his script. He *certainly* knows better, and I am so sorry for any pain or injury this inept, troublemaking boob of a dog . . ."

Well, shoot, I think dejectedly. *Or rather, no shoot. It appears I've done it again. I tried to impress, and instead I've caused a problem, and now my road to the Walk is in a ditch that I'll never escape because . . .*

"Oh that's *hilarious*!" Smirkson doubles over laughing and then grabs his costar's forearm.

"Heart! Did you see? That little pug again thought outside the box and attempted to add more flavor to his small role! He was fancying himself as a gun spinner! Too bad he couldn't quite nail it as it would have been cool for him to spin it like that before giving it to you!

"Maurice!!" He yells over to Matt, again calling him by the wrong name much to the latter's humiliation. "If there's time, maybe have the screenwriter work in a gun spin! That would be swell of you, big guy!"

Both actors guffaw and then give me a little pat on my pug rump. Deborah and Maurice, er Matt, look like they don't know what to make of things but Deborah quickly recovers.

"Yes, that PD is quite the card, isn't he," she says, adding a nervous "teehee" before composing herself. "Well, let's get started, shall we? PD, you will walk in just behind Mr. Heart's character, Galahad. Ralph will stand by with me and observe, and our stand-in, William, will . . . wait, where is William?"

One of Smirkson's aides rushes forward. "I'm sorry, Deborah, I meant to text you. William came down with something last night. We were hoping one of your other bit players here could handle it. It's only a couple of seconds on camera . . .'

Lord, please. Pretty please tell me that Ralph is not—boom!—just like that getting the Bane compadre role. I mean, Marie could dump the hoop skirt and just wear the pantaloons and . . .

"No problem, Susan!" chirps Matt, pausing to give me a smirk. "Ralph the Dog happens to be on hand for any and all open roles. He will be"—another smug smile my way—"a *swell* sidekick. Brenda, bring William's costume and put it on Ralph. Pin where needed." He turns to the leads. "Otherwise, sirs, we are ready when you are."

Our costume director scurries over to dress that scoundrel of a scuzzball as I try to remember when I used my last chit with God and lost my answered-prayer privileges. I'll need to share a Great Auntie Sheila cookie with Mommy and maybe stop hogging the best dog benches at Bark and Boarding's Sunday Funday to gain some God points back. Sadly, I seem all out of favors at the moment.

"Places!" Deborah barks, pulling me out of my pity party. And really, I ask myself, why should little me be sad? This is my second time next to two big movie stars who clearly like me a lot. And I have one of the best roles in the scene! This rising star's Star on the Walk remains on track!

Everyone takes their places. About three dozen bit players and lesser extras are scattered here and there on the arena grounds, serving as townsfolk. Some will be far in the background, while faces the audience knows from the restaurant and town square scenes will scoot closer in on the action as tension rises. Galahad and PD the Pal are just off camera to the right, while Bane and my own personal bane are to the left.

As Deborah bends down to get her clapperboard and the camera operators (four on the ground plus one in a helicopter above us) get ready for the big fight scene to start, your hero PD is battling his own warring thoughts. *What to do?* I think. *Simply hand Galahad the pistol and step aside, becoming just one more unremembered 'friend' of a lead character . . . or again do something to stand out, to make the audience think of PD the Pal whenever they think of this film, and cementing my place in movie history.*

Well, gosh, it's a no-brainer, right? And I have just the plan! Just a tiny thing, nothing that ruins the movie or anything. Just that little *PD touch.* Mommy will be so proud of me when I am getting my Best Supporting statuette. *Do they make a dog-shaped one?* I wonder. *Because . . .*

"CUT!!"

I'm so lost in my Oscar ceremony daydream that I apparently have missed not one, not two, but six claps of the board. The only reason Deborah isn't screaming at me is that her dressing-down would be drowned out by the hysterically laughing stars, who are mimicking me holding a tiny mic and doing an acceptance speech in what I guess is their idea of bark language.

Deborah and Matt both stare daggers at me and then do fakey laughs along with the big guys' real ones.

"Okay, PD, you with us?" Matt says, taking over for the seething Deborah. "Good." As I give him a faux apologetic head hang, he leans toward me and snarls: "Pay. Attention. This. Time. Black. Dog."

Deborah uses her megaphone to address the full crowd. "This take is for film, so give it your best! Let's win Mr. Chewy that Best Picture Oscar!"

I am wondering why all the kissing up about the big boss, but then I see him and a couple of other Chewy Corporation honchos honchoing toward some seats off camera. I'm suddenly very reassured that my decision to add just a dash of salt to my "plain pal" role is the right one. I mean, what choice do I have? I have *got* to impress Mr. Chewy! I have *got* to impress Messrs. Heart and Smirkson! I have *got* to get my Star on the Walk!

My basic, unembellished role is to walk behind Galahad into the center of the arena where Bane and Stinky stand. After Bane says, "How about we end this here and now? Ten paces, Galahad," I am to unholster the pistol I'm wearing and hand it to him. Then I am to nod encouragingly and step out of the shot. Simple.

And altogether unremarkable. Unexceptional. Unmemorable. Not the way a true star-in-the-making would handle the scene. No way! I have to shine! And I have the perfect plan.

In the classic 1987 crime thriller *The Untouchables,* there's a scene where one of Al Capone's thugs sneaks into the home of Sean Connery's character, Jim Malone. The thug is carrying a switchblade. Connery's character laughs and says what became one of the most famous lines from the movie and is now part of our cultural lexicon.

". . . Brings a knife to a gunfight!"

I know *A Bone to Pick* isn't about Prohibition Era crime boss Al Capone being brought to justice by treasury officer Elliot Ness, but I bet this arena scene will have the critics calling PD the Pug the modern-day Malone.

Because . . . Galahad brought a PD to a gunfight!

Everyone is now in place. The main actors appearing in this climactic moment—including yours truly—are just off screen; the bit players and smaller extras are in their preassigned places; the production crew is nearby, ready to jump to if needed; and Mr. Chewy and the honchos are sitting erect, no doubt thinking about how crucial this small section of the film will be for Chewy Productions fortunes, to how quickly (hopefully positive) word of mouth spreads, to how many (hopefully positive) press pieces the movie receives, to how many theaters it ends up in.

Deborah holds the clapperboard aloft, taking a moment to grin at her superior and the other biggies. Mr. Chewy actually gives her a thumbs-up, causing her to beam like I've never before witnessed. Even Matt has a sort of pleasant look on his sourpuss face.

"And *action!*" Deborah yells, banging the film slate. Its sharp *clap!*

jolts us all to attention and as the six cinematographers aim their Panavision digital cameras at us, at the shopkeepers, at the townsfolk, and at various other points around the arena, I have never felt more like showbiz is the only biz for PD. I am in my element, doing what I was born to do, from this day forward bringing entertainment to the masses, a movie star, a movie star, a *movie star!!*

"Psst! PD! Go!," Galahad says, snapping me out of my reverie with a light kick to my pants-covered rump. Out of the corner of my googly left eye, I spy the cameraperson assigned to the big star and little me; Bane and dog bane have their own. As Galahad and I head to meet our enemies in the center of the stadium, I do an exaggerated cowboy walk just to add a bit of PD pizzazz . . . until I see Deborah angrily shaking her head "no" and go back to my regular gait. I look up to see Bane and Ralph now just feet away.

And I know it's now or never if I am going to steal this scene.

Bane parts his lips but before he can even start to deliver the threat that is supposed to kick off the duel, a growl sounds from Black Dog. It starts as a menacing but low-pitched snarl and escalates to a thunderous roar. The shop workers stare wide-eyed and place their shaking hands to their trembling lips; the townsfolk take a frightened step back; Galahad pats the rounded top of his protector's hat as Bane stumbles back with an expression that can only be described as sheer terror. Deborah has never looked so pleased, Mr. Chewy never so impressed. Even Matt gives a slow clap.

Or, wait. Um, maybe it went down a teensy bit differently:

And I know it's now or never if I am going to steal this scene.

Bane parts his lips but before he can even start to deliver the threat that is supposed to kick off the duel, a growl sounds from Black Dog. Galahad trips over the short stout body of his sidekick that has unexpectedly stopped mid stride, stumbling forward and knocking Bane onto Ralph, who decides at that moment to renew our real-life rivalry. He bounds away from Bane, getting inches from my face before doing a loud snarl of his own. Every dog out on a walkie in the vicinity of this movie set joins in, setting off a chorus of barks, yowls, bays, yaps and yelps. The shop workers and townspeople do raise their hands, but it's to cover their ears in annoyance and not to cover their mouths in trepidation.

Deborah has never looked so enraged. Mr. Chewy could not look less impressed. Only Matt is all smiles, tucking his thumb in as he holds up his fingers and stares at me.

"And that's *four*, Dog," he mouths silently, shaking his head.

Assistants race over like their human tails are on fire and pull the stars to their feet. Makeup is touched up, clothing dusted off, queries about well being and the desire to file lawsuits are posed. Deborah is frozen in place, staring at Mr. Chewy, seemingly waiting for this modern-day emperor to give PD a thumbs up or an edict to be fed to the lions.

After apparently getting a subtly sent response, our crimson-hued director turns around.

"PD? Ralph? There isn't time to train new actors for your parts, so Mr. Chewy is letting this go. Our beyond gracious stars, Messrs. Heart and Smirkson said something about 'PD will be PD' and even chuckled a bit, which is lucky for you. Now! You listen to me, PD, no more improv! *Listen* for Bane's challenge and *hand* Galahad the pistol and then both of you *move out of the scene!!* Got it?"

Ralph and I both wag our tails in acquiescence. I am sure he is as relieved as I am for this reprieve. But there is a difference between us. He is a nobody of a gnat of a nothing. I am a rising star. He is forgettable and will never again see a movie set. I potentially have a long and illustrious career ahead of me. But it starts—or ends—with this movie.

I have to be good. I know I do. I dare a glance over at the small seating area, and see Mommy standing at the front of the other spectators, binoculars held up to her pretty Mommy face, probably trying to read Mr. Chewy's lips, to learn whether her little star is still in the film, still a real star in the making. Apparently seeing me staring at her through the binocs, she puts them aside and waves her arms animatedly before hefting a big homemade poster that reads, "PD Needs An Agent!" with her cell number underneath the glittered lettering.

Clap!

"Action!"

Bane: "How about we end this here and now? Ten paces, Galahad."

Galahad: "Black Dog! Hand me my pistol!"

PD, I tell myself, *it's like Miss Sophia telling you to sit, stay, and roll over. Just. Do. The. Command. Then maybe get a treat from a fanny pack! You can do this, you can do this, you can do this . . .*

Except I can't. Not if I want my "treat" to be a Best Supporting Actor statuette.

I think of Clint Eastwood in *Revenge of the Creature,* Sylvester Stallone in *Bananas,* Matt Damon in *Mystic Pizza*—three megastars who started as extras with tiny roles, then went on to become award-winning movie icons. Theirs is the path on which I now tread! *A Bone to Pick* is my maiden movie, to be remembered as the film that launched my career!

Galahad and Bain are as still as statues as the cameras catch the sweat on their brows, the slight tic in their shirts as their hearts beat, the almost imperceptible shaking of their thighs. Galahad is reaching a hand behind him, waiting for me to place the pistol in it; Bain is drawing his own weapon. Ralph, per usual, is a waste of space.

I go to give Galahad the gun. It's in my paw and mere inches from his hand, when . . . my canine protector gene kicks in. *I must protect Mommy! I must protect Mommy! Or this dude; whoever.* The point is, there is no chance my human is going into a fight without my help. And by *help*, I mean I am taking the proverbial—in this case, prop-gun imaginary—bullet.

Somewhere nearby, someone is loudly whispering something over and over. Something like, "Peewee, go have some fun." Or maybe, "Fifi, you're blocking my sun," or perhaps, "Leelee, you're number one." Oh, wait—I guess four's the charm for my hearing:

"PD, GIVE HIM THE GUN!"

Deborah is apoplectic, choleric, fuming. I quickly drop the weapon into Galahad's hand and scurry out of camera-shot. The rivals turn and stand back to back. Karl, who plays the proprietor of the general store, says, "And . . . begin!" and the men start their ten-pace walks. They reach the eighth step when . . .

I glance over at Mommy, who's giving me two big Roger Ebert thumbs-up. As I beam at her with my snagglesmile, some Mommy memories suddenly pop into my head: The time her date was going to put his yucky icky lips on her pretty ones! The time that dog that reminded me of Ralph sniffed her leg! The time that kid came to the door selling chocolate—*chocolate!* We can't have chocolate in the home of a dog! It's toxic to me!

My ancestral genes are screaming, *Protect my human! Help my human! Keep my human safe!*—just like they did the first time some proto-PD ran between his cavemommy and a saber-toothed tiger. *Protect my human! Help my human! Keep my human safe!*

At step ten, the men spin around. Bane holds the pistol high on the grip and points it straight at his rival. Galahad too has his weapon out in front of him, one leg forward, shoulders relaxed, back ramrod straight. *He's got this, he's got this, he's got this.*

But what if he doesn't?

My reptilian brain shoves other parts of PD's noggin aside and slithers into action. I'm no longer in charge of my little pug self. The ancestral dog, the prehistoric dog, ages before domestication, takes over. The next thing I know:

Black Dog bounds forward. Soaring into the air in a leap reminiscent of Buddy in *Air Bud,* I fly into Bane's rigid gun-aiming right arm, knocking the pistol from his hand. The weapon hurtles into the air, then lands smack on top of Ralph's head. Ralph decides he should bury his new "toy," and he starts digging furiously in the dirt, guarding the gun with his body as he does so. Determining that, *no,* it is in fact *my* toy, I pounce on Ralph, and a tug-of-war ensues. Snarling through clenched teeth, we pull and pull, until . . .

Ralph and I fly apart. He crashes into Matt, who had leapt forward when the battle for the toy gun began, and I tumble head over paws into Marie, whose giant lollipop drops to the ground next to me. I am about to sample a lick when suddenly I am again airborne, this time being lifted by the scruff of my neck. I see Ralph is similarly aloft in human hands. I am reminded of our big fight during my short stint as a landscaping assistant that culminated in our being lifted into the air by Hoss and Slim (chapter three of *Working Like A . . . Dog!*).

But this might be worse.

Because while Ralph is in the hands of a fuming Deborah, my furry little nape is being clutched by none other than the man who holds my literal neck in his hands and maybe my professional neck on the chopping block.

Mr. Chewy.

I don't dare a look. I can't. I can't bear to let myself believe this could be it, the end. No Walk of Fame. Just a walk of shame.

But then I hear a voice that affords me a teeny tiny modicum of hope, like that of a governor calling the executioner at 11:59 to halt an execution.

"Hey, Charles," Heart calls to the boss. "Don't be too mad at PD. I think the little guy meant well with his attempt to, uh, 'help' me during the duel. We can edit. The picture will still be great. Let's forgive Black Dog this little black mark."

"Yeah," Smirkson chimes in. "This little goofball dog has made the whole shoot, well, fun. Even if a bit more work and extra takes were needed."

As I am lowered to the ground, I risk a peek at this governor of my fate—and I'm shocked to find a big grin on his face. He winks at me, then addresses the director.

"Figure it out, Deborah. Work with the editors. Shoot the final close-up of Galahad's face. We can use it to tease *A Bone to Pick: Bane's Revenge*. "Nice work, all! I'm off." And, with one more wink my way, Mr. Chewy heads to his just-landed helicopter.

I am so overwhelmed by the seesawing of my emotions over the past several seconds—*Fired? Lawsuit? Prison? Another chance? Still employed?*—that I haven't noticed the two men squatted down next to me.

I look up to see Heart and Smirkson sharing a smile before Heart leans closer to me. Giving my scruff a loving rub, he looks at me and whispers:

"I'll say this about you, PD. You sure put the *extra* in extra."

Chapter Seven

OPENING NIGHT! . . . IT'S OPENING NIGHT!

She was a vision in velvety fawn fur, and the mesmerizing sway of her haunches was making it hard to concentrate on the famous faces around us. I thanked my very lucky stars that she had accepted the invitation and finally was my girl. No longer a secret, my former-ly-called secret fawn girl pug crush was now my swain, my love, my no doubt soon-to-be betrothed. Mrs. PD Pug, née Fawn Girl. Forever and ever starts tonight, and . . .

"PD! PD, snap to! Hold your head up and look like the star you are, for Heaven's sake!"

While she looks so pretty in her midnight-blue gown and matching heels, Mommy is no fawn girl pug. But this sec-ond-choice date will have to do on this monumental occa-sion. Because . . . alas, I didn't see my (okay, still secret and never-spoken-to) true love on any recent walkies, and so I couldn't (hopefully get up the nerve to) ask her to my big movie premiere night.

The large reception space that Mr. Chewy's company has rented for the big event has a good sixty or so white table-cloth-laden tables for eight, spaced comfortably apart. There's a screen in the front of the room, and it's mega huge so even the guests at the far end of the room can easily see the action.

This special showing is just for the cast, the top-tier crew, and a bunch of top Hollywood stars, directors, producers and other industry pooh-bahs who got special courier-delivered fancy-pants invitations from Mr. Chewy. It's the first time the film is being seen by anyone other than the top Chewy executives. Not even Messrs. Heart and Smirkson have as yet viewed themselves on the big, or any, screen. I wonder if they are as nervous as, um, those of us still on the way to fame.

I lead the way to our table, Mommy holding the loop of the midnight-blue velvet leash she had specially made for my big night, its snap hook secured to my matching velvet harness. While Mommy does look pretty in her dress and fancy updo, I know any and all eyes looking our way are focused on *me*, the famous actor. Or soon-to-be-famous, anyway.

The clipboard-holding Chewy woman who is tasked with greeting and seating the guests directs us to table four. Despite feeling nervous, I force myself to walk with a confident strut, head high, eyes straight ahead, resisting the temptation to gawk at all the famous faces in the room.

"Here's our table, sweetie," Mommy says as we reach our place. Seated in the other six chairs are three people I recognize, alongside their guests. Marie is there with a man I assume is her husband. Next to him is Susan—Smirkson's assistant, whom I saw during the set-up for the arena shoot—sitting with an older woman. The third pair is Darla from the butcher shop and a woman who looks so much like her I conclude they must be sisters.

To give the evening a true theater feel, a couple dozen Chewy Productions crew members are dressed in 1930s-style movie usher uniforms, complete with grey and burgundy tailcoats, dark slacks, red-and-black pillbox hats, and dark dress shoes. The ushers are going from table to table, pushing little red carts bearing not only large and small bags of popcorn but also all sorts of movie yummy candies from yesteryear. I salivate as I spy Raisinets, Sugar Babies, Red Vines, Goobers, Dots and more.

Since the food bearers are a few tables away, I take a moment to suck up the bit of drool slowly headed toward the plush white carpet before letting my eyes roam the room. Three tables away—at table one—are just six people. Seated in plush red velvet-covered chairs are Mr. and Mrs. Chewy; Heart and his wife, Suanne; and Smirkson and his wife, Amy. The group is laughing at something Mr. Chewy has just shared.

I try not to be overly obvious as I wriggle and jiggle a bit in my seat, hoping to get noticed by the big shots. I feel a frisson of excitement as Heart turns his head while in mid-giggle—perhaps seeking the source of the bouncy bustle he senses nearby—and catches me gawking his way. I am giddy with self-importance as he wiggle-waves his fingers at me and does an exaggerated wink.

Surreptitiously I peek around, hoping that the whole room is talking about the little black pug who warranted a wiggle-waggle from those famous fingers. Alas, everyone—even Mommy—is focused on a suddenly spot-lit silver stand to the side of the massive movie screen. Atop the stand sits a large silver microphone with the words Chewy Productions in gold on its base.

I watch as Mr. Chewy rises from his seat and takes his place behind the stand. There is a tiny whine from the mic as he does a slight lean forward and begins speaking:

"Ladies and gentlemen," he begins, his eyes panning the large group, "what a magnificent moment this is! What a spectacular spectacle! What a pageant of pageantry! On behalf of all of us at Chewy Productions, I want to personally thank each and every one of you for coming out to celebrate the premiere of what I truly believe is going to wow not only *you*, but also every Oscar voter deciding who is going to get those coveted gold statuettes at the Academy Awards.

"*A Bone to Pick: Vexation Vengeance* is, in my oh-so-humble opinion"—here he pauses to wait for some scattered chuckles and titters—"the best revenge film since *Kill Bill*, reminiscent of *Unforgiven, Death Wish,* even *True Grit.*

"Horace Heart and Dirk Smirkson—"

The mere mention of their names sparks a thunderous round of applause that stretches into a good two or three minutes as every person in the room, minus the stars themselves, of course, rises to make it a standing ovation. I fantasize my name was included, and I am about to jump up on our table and take a bow when Mommy gives my velvet leash a slight tug, pulling my ego back to Earth.

"Thank you all . . . thank you. Horace Heart and Dirk Smirkson have made me and the Chewy Production team proud to be associated with such greats. It is my honor, my undeserved honor, that they signed on to our film. I can only hope they are as pleased with the final product as my team and I are."

"And now . . . let the show begin!"

Mr. Chewy takes a moment to point here and there at people in the audience, doing that "I'm important and know important people" thing, before stepping away from the microphone and retaking his cushy seat.

Moments later is the moment I've dreamed of since the day Mommy got the call saying I was chosen to be an extra. As the room's overhead lights go out and we are momentarily in a pitch-black reception hall, I feel exhilarated to the point of passing out. I distract myself by sneaking some of Mommy's remaining candies—a mini box of Milk Duds and a handful of Swedish Fish—and stuffing them in my maw.

Sugar-sated, I hop a bit in my seat. Then I feel Mommy's soft hand stroking my little paw. I take a moment before the film begins to again thank my stars—Hollywood ones and lucky ones—that Mommy saw the online ad that got me here. I don't think I've felt this special since the time an auto-delivery glitch accidentally sent us two big bags of Natural Farm bully sticks in the same week.

And this is *better!*

And now here we go. I've never sampled alcohol, but I think I might be drunk on euphoria. I glance at Mommy just as she glances at me, and the look on her face is a mixture of pride, astonishment, and so much love. She kisses her fingers and touches them to my head. I think I see a little tear in her eye. I find myself as excited for her to see me on film as I am to see myself.

Well, almost.

The opening credits fill the screen. This is the moment I've dreamed about: I am about to be seen in a movie! *Me!* PD the Pug on the silver screen. This is my breakout role—the background performance that will catapult me to the forefront of the film world. Take notes, other bit players, take notes!

The movie begins. We are on the edge of our seats, watching this tale of revenge, this story of two warriors in a battle—one man led by ego, the other by love: love of his betrothed, love of his business and its financial impact on the small town. The air around me is so tense with both worry and hope for the hero Galahad that it's all I can do not to chomp down the small plain popcorn Mommy set aside for me to eat ("Quietly, PD!") during the action.

The backstory is finished, and all of us are caught up on the reason for the feud. We get closer to the . . . *oh, c'mon already, get to the parts that I am in! Me!* Galahad and Bane are walking into the restaurant. The restaurant! The scene of my first appearance on film. My first step on the way to that Walk of Fame.

I relive the feeling of being on set for the first time, outside the faux restaurant with Matt, waiting to be sent inside to start my stride to stardom. I think of my glee upon learning that I would be at table two, right next to the leads. And, okay, I might also be fondly reliving the food. I can almost taste the chicken, the burger, the spaghetti on my little pink tongue.

Yes, yes, there was the *tiny* issue of my choosing chewing over gasping, and that whole "edit out PD's eating" thing. But any fine method actor often must make decisions in the moment. And, well, eating felt right to me. And to my tummy.

I watch, enrapt, waiting to see the parts featuring yours truly that were left in the restaurant scene. Mommy shushes me as I do a little yip when I spy my paw near the easel-mounted menu board on the floor of the restaurant as Bane looks my way to study the lunch choices. I stare and stare, my googly eyes feeling like they are about to pop out, waiting to see more of PD in the faux food joint.

We see patrons dining, wide shots and close-ups, cooks yelling "Order up!," waitpersons scurrying about, and, finally, Bane doing his end-of-scene snicker. But alas, no more shots of PD.

But that's okay! There's lots more movie to come! Lots more PD to see!

The story on the screen continues. Galahad has expressed his offense over Bane's flirting with Catherine and his attempts to damage Galahad's business reputation in the community.

The gauntlet has been thrown, so to speak, and now we are in the town square. The men are staring one another down in the street while the town otherwise is eerily silent.

My big round eyes scan the makeshift buildings. They linger, of course, on the firehouse. The camera pans past the storefronts, past City Hall, and along the street lined with trees where the occasional bird lands and shares its song. We go to a close-up of the angry face of Galahad, followed by a cut to the "What, me worry?" smirk Bane offers in reply. Then, as if the townsfolk can sense the danger coming, all the doors open as one and the workers exit their shops and the government center. Other citizens appear from off camera, and bodies begin filling the square.

Karl, Steven, Darla, the other proprietors, and the townsfolk are literally larger than life on the giant screen. Their make-up is perfectly applied. Everyone's hair is styled just right. I applaud Brenda in my mind as I note the authenticity of the costumes. The camerawork is superb, the lighting is dramatic, and the editing has maximized the suspense. I watch candy store owner Marie lick her gigantic lolly, the spiral stripes staining her tongue blue.

I wait and wait to see PD the Firepug. I am giddy. I know it'll just be a moment or two before that handsome furry face under the fire helmet fills the screen. I mean, yes, I know, my pouncing on Bane in my attempt to save the town from Bane's almost/sorta fire was edited. But still! I raced out of the firehouse just like everyone else raced out of their buildings! I was concerned just like everyone else! I was a good dog! Good dog!

So. Where. Am. I???

Oooh! There! Look! The camera again slowly pans around the square, ending again on the tense faces of the two combatants. As the camera travels from there to the dusty ground, again capturing the scared looks of the residents, I see it! There it is! A firefighter's black-booted forepaw outside the firehouse! And . . . And . . . no more shots of PD.

But, er…That's okay! Lots more PD to see!

The tale goes on. Soon we are in the arena; we've reached the big showdown, the climax, the fated battle. I look around me at the packed reception room; the safety lighting allows just enough illumination for me to see the whites of wide-open eyes all around me: enthralled viewers, everyone gripped, captivated, completely absorbed in the storyline. Their concern for Galahad, their fear of Bane, is palpable.

And then the big moment arrives. The camera is so close up on Bane that I can see a tiny mole high up on his left cheek that I didn't notice during filming. His eyes narrow; his upper lip rises into a sneer. Next we see our hero. Galahad is stock-still, staring into his enemy's eyes, the only indication of nervousness being a small bead of sweat on his forehead.

"How about we end this here and now? Ten paces, Galahad."

"Black Dog! Hand me my pistol!"

I'm squirming and bouncing so much in my seat that Marie leans over and gives my paw a calming pat. She, too, knows this is my big scene, the scene that launches my movie career into the stratosphere, the scene that my grandpugs and great-grandpugs will remember as the moment their megastar Grandpug went from an unknown to a superstar.

Galahad has asked Black Dog for his weapon. Seconds from now, this premiere audience will see me—*me!*—in my thus far finest acting glory. We are about to see PD the Pug as Black Dog! I excitedly wait to see me on this ginormous screen, the camera capturing my protective, defensive stance, slowly traveling from brown derby hat to my little black boots, pausing just a moment on the frightening-looking weapon in my holster.

There it is! My pistol-holding furry forepaw! Wow! Super close up! Filling the giant screen! My paw! *Mine!* I can't believe this audience, all future audiences, are about to see PD the Pug as Black Dog!

The weapon falls into the waiting human hand. And then . . .

Huh? Suddenly we are to the ten paces part. What happened to Black Dog? Why is the duel such a big deal?? I mean, duel schmuel! Get back to Black Dog! We all want to see more of Black Dog!

Oh. Except we don't. No one besides me, anyway. Even Mommy has her dainty Mommy hand to her cheek, eyes wide, watching Galahad and Bane prepare for the big fight, seemingly having forgotten all about her little PD as Black Dog. I know I'm not being entirely fair; this is, after all—with a deserved bow to Gary Cooper—the *High Noon* moment in this story.

The final scenes are upon us. As I watch the men square off, weapons raised, elbows locked, I think back to filming day in the arena and my *tiny* ad lib, my *teensy* bit of improv, and I give a quick thanks for the magic of editing. But still, you'd think they'd have found a way to give the very important Black Dog a *bit* more screen time . . .

We're almost at the end of the movie. To minimize the chances of leaks to *Hollywood Reporter, Access Hollywood* and other entertainment publications and shows, no one except the actors and crew in the final scene, the director, and a few bigwigs know how the film ends. So I am just as riveted to the screen as Mommy and everyone else here at the premiere.

And it's a cliffhanger for sure. The hero and his villainous counterpart appear seconds away from what is sure to be a bad day for one of them. I pull a deep breath through my flat nose, and it's all I can do not to hold my paws to my eyes. I am so scared—along with the rest of the audience I bet—that Galahad is going down, that evil is going to win out. So what happens next is a big surprise . . .

. . . to probably everyone but Mr. Chewy. I mean the top executive has to think of his bottom line, and that means sequel, right?

The camera now is tight on Bane's trigger finger. It feels like time has stood still all around me. The action on the screen suddenly goes into slomo. Galahad's steady eye, Bane's squeezing finger, the townsfolk—first a wide shot, then a couple tense close-up faces. We all wait for Bane's gun to *Boom!*, its bullet punching into Galahad, the latter's body falling to the arena floor, some spectators racing forward, some fleeing to perceived safety.

But that doesn't happen.

"Bane! Wait."

Galahad lowers his weapon. His shocked adversary slowly does the same. As I watch the tense ending, I realize I still haven't exhaled and expel a little snort-breath. The humans around me look similarly fixated.

"What is it, Galahad? We need to finish this!"

"Yes we do, Bane. But bloodshed, a body in the streets of my town, the good citizens dealing with the aftermath of tragedy is not the way."

"What then, Galahad? What do you propose? Because you're already as dead to me as I am to you."

And then the final scene. A close-up of our hero, Galahad.

"And one of us *will* be dead, Bane. But not *here*, not *now*."

The camera draws closer, Galahad's handsome face filling the gigantic square in front of us. "I'll see you soon, Bane. I'll see you soon."

Fade to black.

The room explodes in applause. Mommy leaps to her feet, along with the hundreds of other premiere audience members, every viewer clearly giving the film the proverbial two enthusiastic thumbs up. Every viewer smiles and cheers. Every viewer is now turning toward table one, where the stars and their brides and the big boss and his missus are the only ones still seated; the two leads rise to accept the warm reception. Mrs. Smirkson looks like she is crying.

Everyone here is pleased as punch.

Everyone here except me, that is.

I am most definitely not pleased. I am displeased, discontented, disappointed. Just, well, *dissed.*

That's *it?* That's my part in this movie? A forepaw in the restaurant? A hind paw in the town square? Another forepaw dropping a gun into Galahad's hand in the arena? Nothing more than my little furred feet?

As I am staring down at the paws that are apparently are the only film-worthy PD parts, Mommy takes one in her pretty manicured hand and strokes my head. She's leans to my ear and is about to whisper one of her Mommy "It's okay, PD" lines when the closing credits begin to roll. In respect to the performers, crew, and everyone associated with this production, we join the room in silence and give the screen our attention.

In ginormous type, first the film title, then the names of the film's two stars fill the screen one at a time, each remaining up for a good five seconds:

A Bone to Pick: Vexation Vengeance

Horace Heart

Dirk Smirkson

Next are the other known and semi-known names, the more famous getting their own moment of glory for a second or two. Lesser-knowns follow, grouped in threes. Then the rest of the cast names begin rolling up the screen. I wiggle a bit in my seat when I see my candy store pal Marie's name appear. *I know her!* I think. *She dressed me!* We reach the bottom of the cast names and then there is a bit of black, and then another full screen for the executive producer, and one for our executive director, Deborah.

Next, other important and semi-important crew member names roll. There's costume designer Brenda; the music composer; the editors; the set designer; the writers. There's Matt's name, followed by his assistant (*assistant!*) director title. More and more people and positions (there's a *second* and *third* director? You can get lower than Matt?) are recognized. So many names! Five personal assistants to Mr. Heart and as many to Mr. Smirkson. Other roles like music composer, casting director, location scout, visual effects editor, stuntman coordinator, stuntmen, hair and makeup director, grip, second grip, the catering company. On and on it goes.

Then special recognitions and thanks. Shooting locations. Logos for guilds, unions, equipment sponsors. Names of government agencies that gave Mr. Chewy's company tax credits or other perks for use of a locality. And then another long pause before a full screen is given to the words "A Chewy Productions Film."

It's all there. On the big screen. All those names, all the names of everyone who helped make this film. All of them.

All except the one name I care about. Mine.

I hang my pug head in shame. I can't look at Mommy. I can't look at Marie who is seated just two chairs away from us. I certainly can't look toward Matt's table, wherever it is, can't bear to witness the cruel smirk I am sure he'd give me. I can't look anywhere but down.

Mommy pats my little paw on my armrest. Assuming it's time to go, I move to get my furry fanny up from the soft seat, but that's not what she wants.

"PD! Look!" She exclaims, pointing excitedly and bouncing in her chair. "Look, sweetie!"

I slowly raise my head and look at the screen, that wicked screen that betrayed me, ignored me, embarrassed me. And I'm stunned with both shock with glee.

While I had hung my head, the Chewy logo had disappeared and then a brief final recognition filled the screen, words that make my little pug googly eyes double in size, were it possible.

Also contributing to this Chewy Productions film:

PD the Pug

I stare at the screen. At *me, me, me!*

And then another full screen of just the Chewy logo. A big smiley dog.

And . . . Fade to black.

The Chewy dog isn't the only delighted dog. Sure, I mean, yes, by the time you reach the end of the credits, a theater is mostly cleared out. But no matter.

I'm a star. PD the Pug is a *Star.*

Also contributing to this film:
PD THE PUG

EPILOGUE

The cardboard poster mocks me, its glued-on glitter now just a bunch of rainbow-hued sprinkles on the white living room rug. The "PD Needs An Agent!" in huge letters above the close-up photo of my furry face reminds me anew that no Hollywood rep has called the phone number Mommy posted under my mug. No talent booker, no magazine writer, no entertainment show host, no dog product executive needing an endorser. No calls. No one wants me.

After *A Bone to Pick* hit theaters last month and everyone— well, everyone who stayed until the house lights come on and the usher starts cleaning soda-sticky floors, sweeping up buttery popcorn, prying chewed gum off the undersides of seats—saw my name in the credits, I knew it would be just a matters of days, just a week or two until the biggest of the biggie Hollywood talent agencies were bidding against one another for the privilege of adding that dog with the famous paws to their roster of clients.

But a month later, I remain agent-less. Magazine and TV show Interview-less. Product endorsement-less. I feel as plain and ordinary as the nearly glitter-less poster before me.

Mommy calls to me from the kitchen and I hear kibble rain into my bowl. I'm so morose I haven't even noticed it's mealtime. Which is saying something.

I slowly get up from the carpet, giving one more glance at the poster board. My face, the happy PD picture Mommy chose from the thirty or so "publicity" shots she took of me in the pretty grassy area near our neighborhood gazebo, stares back at me with a "Hollywood Bound!" expression of hope I no longer feel.

As I head to my little food bowl, its exterior decorated all the way around with alternating black and fawn pugs, I notice the ottoman-laden pile of dog acting coach and agent brochures and pooch promotion paraphernalia Mommy collected from the sponsor products table during filming. I muster up a tad bit of courage to believe in myself, grab a pamphlet in my jaws and drop it at her feet, and then bite onto the hem of her jeans and give a tug.

"What is it, little PD?" she asks. "Do you still have the acting bug?" She pats my head. "Tell you what: How 'bout you enjoy your lunch while I give these brochures and ads a looksie? How does that sound?"

Hooray for Mommy! I think, feeling more optimistic as I scamper over to my bowl. As I take my standard two minutes or so to gobble down my kibble, Mommy sits on one of the two kitchen-area cuddle chairs and puts her feet on the ottoman. In her lap are fifteen or so brochures, ads and cards that just might lead to (more!) PD fame. She peruses each and then pats the seat next to her, inviting me to join her.

When I've done my signature triple spin to get myself in a comfy prone position, my head on her lap, I excitedly wait for her to explain her plan to get us on the path to Promotionville.

"Okay, movie star doggie," she muses, playing with my velvety little ear, "let's see what we've got here. I've got a press release from a movie gossip magazines saying they are, quote, 'always looking to report on up-and-coming dog actors'; two brochures from local dog talent representatives; three business cards from the larger national dog star scouts; a pamphlet for a new dog toy whose manufacturer is seeking, quote, 'the new face of Zippy Yippy Yapping Dog: the dog toy that zips and yips'; a couple advertisements for . . ."

I can zip, Mommy! I can yip! I think, jumping off the cuddle chair and then alternating between racing round and round the kitchen island and standing still and loudly yipping over and over.

Mommy's hands fly to her ears before shushing me and picking up her phone. "Sit still and I'll put this on speaker. But PD? No yipping! No noise! Let's be as professional as you will need to be when you're the face of Zippy Yippy or being interviewed for *Dog Fancy*, okay?"

I do one final Olympic race–worthy sprint around the island and then channel Miss Sophia, imagining her holding a treat aloft and saying "Sit, PD! Sit!" I will myself to be quiet and do nothing to distract Mommy as she makes calls that could help get my Hollywood Walk star back on schedule.

"Hmmm, let's start with the Zippy Yippy people," she says, picking up her cell. She taps the numbers, puts the speaker on, and holds the phone a few inches from her mouth. She winks at me as the connection is made and a recording begins.

"Welcome to Zippy Yippy Yapping Dog Company! We put the joy of Zip and Yip into the day of every dog! To place an order, press 1. To check on the status of an order, press 2. To reach an operator, press 0 anytime during this message. If you have a furry friend in search of fame who wants to be the new international face of Zippy Yippy's Yapping Dog toy, press 9."

Mommy shoos me away as I try to press 9 with my too-big-for-the-buttons paw and then taps it herself. We both wiggle around a bit waiting for someone to answer.

"Talent department! This is Betsy. Tell me about your dog star!" an animated voice enquires.

Mommy straightens her posture and speaks in that anchor-type voice she uses in her television and audio work:

"Good morning, I'm PD the Pug's Mommy, and I . . ."

"Peter the Thug—now *that* is a darling dog name! Have I seen him in gansta rap videos? I know they like to have tough-looking dog actors in spiked collars in those. *Ah!* I remember him now! He was with Snoop in that big Rap City Music Channel video that started airing last month, right? I *looooooooved* it!"

"Er, um," Mommy begins. "PD the Pug. Like . . . capital P, capital D. You might have seen him in the smash hit movie *A Bone to Pick: Vexation Vengeance.* PD was—"

"Ooooooh! Horace Heart's latest blockbuster? I *loooooove* him! *Soooo* handsome! I've watched *A Bone to Pick* four times already! Hmmm, though, I can't recall Heart's character having a dog. Remind me?"

Mommy looks at me and takes a breath. "Yes, it was little PD's first-ever movie, but he had some *really* important parts! His forepaw was in the restaurant scene when Bane looks at the menu board. And his back foot was in that tense part in the town square! PD was the firepug! That was his little foot in the firepug boot! And his forepaw was in the big climax scene, too Remember the paw that dropped the gun into Galahad's hand? That was PD's!!"

Betsy goes quiet for so long that I worry we were disconnected. But then I hear a long inhalation.

"PD's Mommy, I so *loooooooove* that you called! Maybe, um, call again in a few years when PD has some more acting under those, um, widely seen paws. But I do have good news you will *loooooooove!*"

Mommy's expression quickly changes from frowny to smiley as she lunges toward the ottoman for the pen and pad. "Great! Is there another toy you are auditioning for?" . The excitement in her voice makes me want to do another Usain Bolt bolt around the kitchen island.

"Erm, not exactly! But *just* for calling, we are going to send PD a free Zippy Yippy Yapping Dog toy! Guaranteed to put the joy of zip and yip in his day! Now I am going to place you on a brief hold, and then our operator will take down your address. You will *looooooove* your Zippy Yippy Yapping Dog! Bye-bye!"

Mommy's pout has returned and she is about to tap the button ending the call when I give her a look that conveys we at least should get my free toy after that depressing conversation. She nods, spends the next five minutes on hold, and then gives the operator the information. I feel the way I do when I want a bully stick but get a dental chew instead. I mean, I got *something*, but it's a far cry from what I asked for.

"Chin up, PD!" Mommy says, perking up and grinning at me. "We have lots more places to call! That was Zippy Yippy's loss. If they say you need more recognition, then let's get you that recognition! Interviews! An agent! A spokesdog gig! Right, PD?"

I spin in circles in solidarity, excitedly imagining myself gaining more notoriety, more fame, more renown, and, ultimately, that Star on the Walk. And it all starts with the next call. The call that just went through!

"Good morning, Famous Furries Talent Agency. I'm Stuart. Who's the soon-to-be famous furry you are calling to tell me about?"

Mommy's hopeful countenance is fully back. "Hey there, Stuart! I am Mommy to PD the Pug! PD already has some fame! He was in the movie that's all the rage in theaters around the world right now, *A Bone to Pick: Vexation Vengeance.* I'm sure you've seen it . . ."

"Yes, of course! It was fabulous! Chewy Productions deserves an Oscar nomination for that one! But . . . hmm . . . I don't seem to remember a PD in it . . . Ah! Was he the very hirsute man who played the proprietor of the general store? Maybe Chewy had a dog playing a human role? Stranger things have happened in film, right? Ha-ha."

Mommy gives me her "Is this guy a nut?" look, then turns back toward her cell. "No, that was Karl Buxley. I guess he is a bit, er, shaggy. But no, PD was the little pug in three *very* important scenes! He was . . ."

She again recites my foot placements, forcing more confidence into her voice than one might feel when trying to get a little-known dog a big agent. Trying to get me signed to a national talent agency based on little more that being a thrice-seen paw in this month's top grossing film.

"Sooooo, your pug was a foot in a film? Is that what you are telling me?" Stuart now sounds decidedly less enthusiastic; the schmoozy agent tone is largely gone. "PD's Mommy, we appreciate your calling, but . . . wait. I have a thought."

Mommy again reaches for her notepad, ready to hear his idea as to other sources for dog star representation. Alas . . .

"My twelve-year-old nephew, Stan, does watercolors of dogs for fifteen dollars. He might be willing to—as a favor to me—paint PD and post it on his Instagram. It might help PD get seen. Stan has, like, *sixty* followers! I mean, most are family or school friends, but you never know; a big agent might stumble upon it!"

Mommy looks gobsmacked. Her eyes travel from me to the phone and back again. Finally she takes a very frustrated breath before addressing this agency screener who clearly has no intention of even making a note about her darling PD to share with the Famous Furries talent team.

"Stuart, I'm grateful for your suggestion, but PD already has a nice headshot. We are looking for an agent, not a painting, but thanks. Have a nice day!"

As the call ends, I remind myself it's still early in the game. Surely *someone* is going to recognize the brilliant performer that is one Mr. PD the Pug and scoop me up—for agency representation, for endorsement deals, for commercials, for event performances, for photo ops at ribbon cuttings, for photos with attendees at trade shows, for appearances to create buzz about new products. The possibilities are limitless! But my options will be very *limited* until Mommy gets that first 'yes.'

Which she will! This is *Me* we are talking about! And, yay! She is making another call!

"*Canine Celebrity Magazine,* where we scoop the poop about America's most celebrated celebrity dogs! This is Isabella. May I help you?"

"Hi! I am PD the Pug's Mommy, and I . . ."

"Who?"

"PD the Pug? He is in the newly-released big hit movie *A Bone to Pick: Vexation Vengeance.* He—"

"Yep. I loved that flick! PD *who?*"

"PD the Pug. His paws were in the film three times, and—"

Click.

Mommy looks wounded as she stares at her phone for a moment and then quickly re-centers herself, no doubt more for me more than for herself. The clock ticks past noon as she grabs a granola bar from the snack cabinet and then gets me a little piece of dog cookie. Both of us reenergized, she sifts through the remaining brochures, ads, cards and press pieces. She gives me a slightly weak smile as she picks up the business card at the top of the paper pile.

"PD? Honey? I want you to keep your little chin up, because there are more places that might help us, okay? I'm not giving up getting you a seat on the fame train! But, sweetie, we do need to be reasonable and accept that you are not Pug Heart or Pug Smirkson. You are PD the restaurant paw, PD the firepug paw, PD the arena paw. *Important* paws on an *important* pug, but the people we are calling don't yet know you, okay?"

I stare at Mommy like she has two heads. I'm PD the *Pug*! PD the *Paw*! Of *course* they all know me!!!

I jump up next to her in the cuddle chair to peek at the notepad on which she is furiously scribbling. I catch "climax scene paw"; "patted on head twice by Horace Heart"; "special recognition in the closing credits"; "full screen with just his name"; "always obedient" (moments later scratched out); "available for events and openings"; and other PD attributes she seems to think might get the attention of an agent, a dog product CEO, an entertainment reporter—someone who could get my famous paw the next foothold on my path to stardom.

Mommy sits up straighter as she taps the next phone number. She sets the phone on the leg I'm lying against, puts it on speaker, and turns the volume up.

"Famous Fido Talent House, where we make your dog a household name. How may I direct your call?"

"Good afternoon! This is PD the Pug's Mommy. I read you represent movie star dogs, and PD is well on his way! You may have seen him in the smash hit *A Bone to Pick*. His was the paw that drops the pistol into Galahad's hand in the arena scene, and—"

Click.

"Tummy Yummy Dog Treats, Jeremy speaking. May I help you?"

"Yes, thank you, Jeremy. I read you are seeking a well-known canine to be the spokesdog for Tummy Yummy. Well, let me tell you about my little pug, PD! His are the paws that everyone is talking about! The paws in those three crucial, pivotal scenes in *A Bone to Pick* that—"

Click.

"Good afternoon, *Distinguished Dog Weekly*. This is Marissa. How may I assist you today?"

"Hi, Marissa! If you are looking for a dog for next month's cover story, have I got one for you! I am the Mommy of PD the Pug, the overnight sensation you no doubt saw in *A Bone to Pick*! He—"

Click!

"Star-Bound Dog Agency, where superstardom for your dog is in the stars! What can I do for you this afternoon?"

"Good afternoon to you! I'm PD the Pug's Mommy. He is the dog getting lauded for his over-the-top performance in *A Bone to Pick*, and . . ."

"Oh great! Your PD was lauded? Hmmm . . . remind me . . . Did he guest on one of the late-night shows? Which one?"

"Er, well, hasn't been on any shows *yet*, but—"

Click!

"Gossip Dog Blog, Davina speaking. What dog dirt can your famous dog dish up for our readers?"

"Hi Davina! My dog, PD, is nearly famous! The *nearly* famous PD the Pug whose paws appeared in—"

Click!

"Doggie Dental Dog Pet Insurance. This is smiley Sam. How can I help you?"

"Yes, Sam. I'm PD the Pug's Mommy. I hear you are looking for known dogs to be the grinning pooches in your insurance ads. Well, my PD has the cutest snaggletooth smile! And his were the famous paws in the new movie *A Bone to Pick!* He would get lots of new customers for Doggie Dental, and—"

Click!

. . . Click!

. . . Click!!!!!

It's now five in the afternoon. Mommy is stroking my little round head as she looks over the handful of remaining places to call: agencies seeking D-listers; magazines with D-listers on the cover, and products endorsed by, yep, D-listers. (For the non-stars out there, the D is not for *dog*, but rather a grading system of sorts indicating the level of a celebrity's celebrity. D-listers are the ones you see on bottom-of-the-barrel reality shows, and in those tabloids with UFOs on the cover, and endorsing shampoo in the circulars you find at Giant Food Store where Mommy gets groceries.)

Shuffling through her pile of brochures, magazines, and clippings, Mommy reaches for a press piece headlined "We Rep ANY Dog! Competitive Rates!" She reads on:

"BigWig Dog can take your dog from no-name to mega fame! We will represent any canine who has appeared in at least one commercial or show or advertisement. And the best part? You keep twenty percent of the fee! Think what you can buy your fur baby with All That Money!! *Twenty* percent!"

Mommy gives me a head rub as she picks up her phone and taps in one more phone number. She puts the phone on speaker and takes a deep breath, preparing to repeat the speech she has perfected over this long, so far fruitless, day . . .

And then hits "end." She sets the cell down and lifts my chin toward her face.

"PD? Sweetie? Listen, I know we didn't get a bite today. But the movie only just came out. Those precious black paws will get noticed. Lots and lots of moviegoers will wonder whose cute little feet have walked their way right into their hearts! It will happen! Agents, dog food company presidents, and entertainment shows . . . you'll see. My phone will be ringing like crazy in no time!"

I wiggle my head, faking enthusiasm I sure don't feel. The reality is no one wanted me today. Not Zippy Yippy, not Famous Furries . . . I bet BigWig Dog wouldn't give us even *five* percent of fees. I'm a paw. Just a paw. I wish the phone hadn't been on speaker today. At least that way I could *pretend* Mommy was getting lots of yeses instead of one hang-up after another.

Somehow sensing my sadness, Mommy sets all the papers aside and lifts me to her chest, snuggling me close. She opens her mouth, no doubt to say some encouraging Mommy words, when her cell buzzes on the ottoman next to us. She lifts it and stares at the screen.

"Hmmmm . . . 'Unknown caller'," she says, frowning a little. "I don't like to answer these, but let's see what they are selling this time, PD." She sets me down next to her and taps the green button. "Hello?"

"Hey, PD's Mom. It's Horace Heart. I hope you don't mind my getting your number from that assistant director, Maurice."

Mommy sits bolt upright. "Um, er, uh, no, not at all, Mister Heart! Wow, um . . Wow! I, er . . . ." Mommy is stammering like a teenager at a Taylor Swift concert. I press my paw into her leg and will her to stop spluttering and gibbering.

"So sorry to bother you," he goes on, "but . . . well, Dirk and I were talking. The movie is going so well that Chewy Productions already is talking about not only the anticipated sequel but perhaps a prequel after that. And there's even buzz about a spin-off TV show."

Mommy looks both pleased and perplexed. "Well, big congratulations to you and Mr. Smirkson, sir, but . . . why are you sharing this with us?"

Mr. Heart takes a breath, and I think I discern a smile in his voice as he tells us the reason for the call.

"Well, Chewy did a poll of moviegoers. Turns out that eighty-three percent of *A Bone to Pick* viewers want Galahad to have a dog friend in the sequels. Now, mind you, it would be just a very tiny role in a couple of scenes. But . . . if you would consider letting PD audition for the role of Black Dog, Dirk and I would put in a good word for you. We love the little guy."

Mommy cuddles me to her, holding me tighter than I remember her ever doing. She kisses my head before thanking Mr. Heart for the audition opportunity, and they end the call.

"Now, PD, it's just an audition," she says, staring into my happy face. "And it's just a teeny role, and there's no guarantee you'll get it . . ." She looks more intently at me and adds: "We need to be prepared for the possibility that another dog will be chosen. But you know what?"

I stop thinking of my maybe-back-on-track stardom and gaze at her pretty face, wondering why she looks so thoughtful, why she has that caring Mommy look about her.

"PD, you might never get an agent. You might never get to be a spokesdog for a dog product. You might never be the cover dog on a dog magazine. You might never get that Star on the Hollywood Walk of Fame. But you know what? You shine brighter than any star in silly Hollywood or even in all the heavens."

My googly eyes search hers.

"PD?," she says, her eyes filling with tears. "You are the star of my *heart* and of my whole *life*."

She squeezes me to her.

"We can audition for Black Dog. Or not. But know this: no amount of fame could ever make you a bigger star than you already are to me."

I want to protest. I want to say *No! I am Black Dog! I have to get my Star! I have to be famous!*

But as I look at Mommy, it hits me that I don't.

I already am a big star in the only way, the only place that truly matters.

I am a star to *Mommy.* I entertain Mommy all day, every day with more drama, comedy, and action (hopefully not too much horror or crime) than anything I could ever hope to do on screen—silver, LED, or any other. I make her *happy.* I make her *smile.*

I'm Mommy's Star. Who needs Hollywood?

(But, folks? I'm still auditioning for Black Dog . . .)

GET IN TOUCH WITH PD!

You can write to him at

PD the Pug Productions
2200 Wilson Boulevard
Suite 102-265
Arlington, VA 22201

Or give him a shout at

pdthepug@gmail.com

ABOUT THE AUTHOR

In late 2021, PD the Pug wowed the literary world with the publication of his debut book, *Get Me Out of Here! Reflections of PD the Put-Upon Pug.* The next two years saw the release of two more PD the Pug masterpieces: *No, YOU Sit! PD the Pug's Manual for How To Train Your Human* and *Working Like A . . . Dog! PD the Pug in Corporate America.* All PD books follow the shenanigans of the world's favorite and funniest "misunderstood" pug who thinks he knows best but who always gets his comeuppance after causing, then somehow overcoming, one hilarious mess after another.

As this fourth book went to press, PD was seen knocking his big round face against Mommy's laptop over and over as he worked on his acceptance speech for the Pulitzer he is just positive will finally come this time. He fully intends to be named first-ever canine winner of this esteemed award.

But with or without such recognition, PD certainly has an impressive resume. Among his many accomplishments, PD holds a Certification of Achievement for (miraculously) passing Puppy One training class. He has been named top dog for number of headfirst landings while attempting to chase a squirrel up a tree; he is, bar none, the best at pooping on the clear-other-end of the dog park from where Mommy is standing with the poop bag; and he has been recognized as a top tail chaser, once spinning an impressive seventeen times in a row before demanding a treat. Impressively, as a puppy he won the highly coveted Pee Award for tipping over while urinating against a bush.

Five years after gracing this Earth with his birth, this descendant of a breed that once was the treasured companion of Chinese royalty still is stunned and amazed that, instead of a castle, he somehow finds himself living in an Arlington, Virginia townhouse with his funny, smiley beloved Mommy.

You can visit PD online at PDThePugProductions.com and get in touch with him at pdthepug@gmail.com. You also can follow him at pd.the.pug on Instagram and Facebook.

A Star Is Born! is PD's fourth book.

ABOUT MOMMY

Mommy Marilee Joyce is privileged to have her own room in PD the Pug's Arlington, Virginia home.

Her PD jobs including feeding, walking and bathing him; cleaning the goopies out of his googly eyes; picking up his poopies; and Q-tipping his ears and nose folds. She is tasked with calming him when he sees his reflection in the sliding glass door and thinks it's another pug trying to get in and steal his bully sticks and toys, as well as making it clear that it won't be too many more minutes before he gets yet another cookie.

Marilee is the owner of Joyce Communications in Washington, DC and PD the Pug Productions. She has served as an anchor and reporter for several television affiliates. In Washington, she has produced and hosted several television programs from Capitol Hill, and her company currently offers full video and audio production services.

Mommy is grateful to God each new morning to have been blessed with PD. And she is amazed that her silly little trouble-seeking nutcase PD is so brainy. She hears he is busy at work on his fifth book . . .

OTHER WORKS BY PD THE PUG

Get Me Out Of Here! Reflections of PD the Put-Upon Pug

No, YOU Sit! PD the Pug's Manual for
How to Train Your Human

Working Like A . . . Dog! PD the Pug in Corporate America

Made in the USA
Columbia, SC
14 October 2024

43565645R00087